GRADE
K

Fluency FIRST!™

Daily Routines to Develop Reading Fluency

Timothy Rasinski • Nancy Padak

 **Wright Group**

The McGraw·Hill Companies

www.WrightGroup.com

 **Wright Group**

Fluency First! Daily Routines to Develop Reading Fluency: Kindergarten
Copyright ©2005 Wright Group/McGraw-Hill

Created by Kent Publishing Services, Inc.
Designed by Signature Design Group, Inc.
Illustrations by Shirely Beckes and Nelle Davis

The publishers would like to acknowledge the authors and publishers of the following copyrighted works, which appear in *Fluency First!* Grade K Teacher's Guide. Page 38, "Husha" and "Sh, Sh, Sh" by Sonja Dunn; page 48, "Hard at Work" by Sonja Dunn; page 72, "Houses" and "Casitas" by Tony Johnston, from My Mexico, Mexico Mio, by Tony Johnson, Penguin Group (USA) Inc.; page 88, "Yam Is Yummy" and "Grandma Makes Me Plantain Flakes" by Uzo Unobagha, from Off to the Sweet Shores of Africa, by Uzo Unobagha, Chronicle Books.

The publisher has made every effort to trace ownership of all copyrighted material and to secure necessary permissions to reprint literature selections. In the event of any question arising as to the use of any material, the publisher, while expressing regret for any inadvertent error, will be happy to make necessary corrections.

Printed in the United States of America.

Send all inquiries to:
Wright Group/McGraw-Hill
P.O. Box 812960
Chicago, IL 60681

ISBN: 1-4045-2671-4
10 9 8 7 MAZ 6 5 4 3 2

Table of Contents

Introduction

Teacher's Notes

Table of Contents continued

Appendix

Building Skills and Strategies

Assessment Black-line Masters

Bibliography

Welcome to Fluency First!

Fluency First! is based on a daily, instructional program proven to show dramatic gains in student's reading fluency, word recognition skills, and comprehension. The program is based on a carefully researched instructional model, the Fluency Development Lesson (FDL). The FDL was created and researched by Drs. Timothy Rasinski and Nancy Padak of Kent State University. Using engaging, motivating reading selections that students practice and perform, *Fluency First!* provides a simple, brief, and effective daily routine to build fluent, confident readers.

What is Fluency?

Reading fluency is the ability to read accurately, automatically, and with meaningful expression. Fluency comprises many of the literacy skills readers acquire as they master decoding skills. Achieving accuracy in decoding is not enough for students to maintain steady growth toward full literacy (Chall, 1996b). Instruction in fluency has been proven to help students bridge the gap between learning to decode and reading for meaning.

Why Fluency First! Works

Fluency First!, based on the Fluency Development Lesson (Rasinski, Padak, Linek, & Sturtevant, 1994), utilizes research-tested activities and teaching techniques in a simple, daily instructional routine that includes:
- brief reading selections
- fluency modeling
- choral reading
- reading-while-listening
- daily repeated readings
- paired reading
- oral recitation with guidance and feedback
- parent involvement
- performance

The Fluency Development Lesson was singled out in the *Report of the National Reading Panel* as an effective instructional model.

…guided repeated oral reading procedures that included guidance from teachers, peers, or parents had a significant and positive impact on word recognition, fluency, and comprehension across a range of grade levels.

About the Authors and Research of Fluency First!

Dr. Timothy Rasinski and Dr. Nancy Padak have been professors and researchers in reading education for over 20 years. For the past decade, they have been leading figures in the research on fluency. Their research has proven that fluency is a key component in successful reading development, and their work has been cited by numerous studies and organizations. In addition to their teaching and research, they have also published articles and books on effective reading instruction and have co-edited the *Reading Teacher*, 1993–99, and are currently co-editing the *Journal of Literacy Research*.

Timothy Rasinski

Timothy Rasinski has been a Professor of Education at Kent State University since 1988. Tim earned his Ph.D. in Educational Theory and Practice at Ohio State in 1985. Tim was an elementary Title I and classroom teacher. At Kent State, Tim directs the university's award winning reading clinic. His scholarly interests include working with children who struggle in reading, family literacy, word study, and reading fluency. Tim is currently a member of the International Reading Association Board of Directors and is a Past-President of the College Reading Association.

Nancy Padak

Nancy Padak is a Distinguished Professor of Education at Kent State University, where she also serves as Project Administrator for the Ohio Literacy Resource Center and directs KSU's Reading and Writing Development Center. Nancy received an Ed.D. from Northern Illinois University in Reading. She worked as a public school teacher and administrator. Her scholarly interests center on supporting teachers' efforts to provide effective literacy instruction, adult and family literacy, and issues related to school-based reform in literacy education. She was named a KSU Distinguished Scholar in 2000 and Distinguished Professor in 2002. Nancy is a Past-President of the College Reading Association

About the Research

Research efforts into improving reading fluency and general reading performance through fluency training have enjoyed a resurgence in recent years.

- Dowhower (1987, 1994) found that the gains made in word recognition, reading rate, and comprehension through repeated readings of one text transferred to passages unfamiliar to the reader.
- Research by Dowhower (1987), Herman (1985), and Rasinski (1990a) demonstrated the facilitative effects of repeated readings on readers' fluency, comprehension, and overall reading achievement.
- Carbo (1978), Chomsky (1976), and Pluck (1995) found that listening to a tape-recorded version of a text had facilitative effects on poor readers' performance. Carbo reported that learning-disabled elementary grade students listening to tape-recorded books while reading the same texts made average gains of 19 months in word recognition after only nine months of instruction.

Rasinski, Padak, Linek & Sturtevant (1994) developed the Fluency Development Lesson, a well-articulated model of fluency instruction that

(a) could be readily integrated into the regular reading curriculum

(b) employed an extensive array of principles implemented over the course of a school year

(c) used several quantifiable measures of reading performance to evaluate the treatment.

Subjects for their study came from second-grade classrooms in elementary schools in a large, urban, ethnically diverse school district. Two classrooms from each school were used. In one classroom, the teacher used the experimental FDL treatment. In the other, the teacher implemented a control treatment. In all comparisons of pre and post test results save one, treatment effects favored the experimental treatment. Analysis to assess the statistical significance of the gains attributed to the experimental treatment indicated that all groups made significant improvement over time on each dependent variable. Students receiving the FDL made considerable gains in their ability to recognize words successfully, that is, quickly and accurately, the hallmarks of automatized reading.

In addition to the quantitative data reported in the study, experimental group teachers noticed significant improvements in students' reading performance and attitude. These improvements were greater than expected when compared with previous years. The teachers attributed the above-average improvements to the Fluency Development Lesson.

In addition to the specific instructional strategies such as modeled reading, assisted/choral reading, and repeated readings embedded in the FDL, one reason for its positive effects is the considerable amount of connected discourse reading engaged in by students participating in the lesson. Although texts are short, the intense rereading in the FDL leads to abundant opportunities for supportive and contextual reading.

The fact that the FDL is an instructional routine independent of any other instructional approach, system, or material, and that it takes a relatively small amount of time to complete, makes it a valuable complement to nearly any major approach to or philosophy of reading instruction.

Utilizes a Simple, Daily Instructional Routine

Drs. Rasinski and Padak provide a program in which the latest research on fluency can be integrated into your curriculum. *Fluency First!* provides simple yet effective fluency instruction for the entire year. Only 10 to 15 minutes of whole-class or group instruction is required per day to realize gains in reading fluency. *Fluency First!* provides everything needed to seamlessly incorporate fluency instruction into your daily routine.

Teacher's Notes Support Implementation of Daily Routine

Teacher's Notes—"Pancakes"

DAY 3

Introduce and Discuss

"Pancakes" provides students an opportunity to practice fluent, rhythmic reading.

Introduce—Direct students to the selection on page 14, or display it using chart paper or a transparency. Take a show of hands of what students had for breakfast today (e.g., cereal, toast, eggs, bagel, fruit, pancakes). List the results of the poll on the board.

Ask Questions—Ask students to name the steps in frying an egg. Tell them that you are going to share a poem that describes how to make pancakes.

Evoke Mood and Feeling—Have students describe how they feel when they eat pancakes. Ask them to explain what pancakes taste like. Write the words on the board and read them to the students.

Model Read and Read Together

Prosody—Read the selection several times. Point to the words as you read. Emphasize the beginning word on each line. On subsequent readings accelerate your reading slightly as you move through the poem.

Choral Reading—Move from modeling the poem to choral reading with students. After three or four readings, invite students to read the poem with you. Read it chorally several times, encouraging students to read it with louder and more expressive voices with each reading. Soften your own voice as students develop mastery of the poem.

Practice—Divide the class into small groups and assign each group one line. Then perform the poem with each group reading their line. Encourage students to rehearse the selection at home with family members and friends.

Related Reading—If students are progressing well, introduce "More Pancakes." As with the first poem, move from modeling the poem to choral reading with students. Read it using the same expression used in the initial selection.

Pancakes

Mix the pancake,
Stir the pancake,
Pop it in the pan.
Fry the pancake,
Toss the pancake,
Catch it if you can.

Christina Rossetti

How did I read?
☺ ☺ ☺

14 Fluency First!

A Related Selection
More Pancakes

Butter the pancake,
Syrup the pancake,
Put it on your plate.
Smell the pancake,
Taste the pancake,
I'm sure I could eat eight!

Tim Rasinski

28 Fluency First!

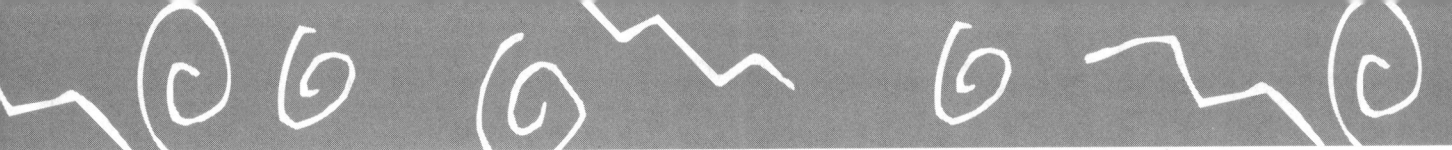

1 Introduce and Discuss

Introduce a reading selection that students will practice and perform.

2 Model Read and Read Together

Read the selection to students modeling fluent and expressive reading. Then read it chorally several times with students.

3 Coach and Rehearse

The next day, coach students as they practice and rehearse their interpretation of the selection.

4 Build Skills and Strategies

Conduct skill-building activities to develop word recognition and comprehension skills.

5 Perform and Celebrate

At week's end, celebrate reading achievement as students perform selections for peers and other members of the school community.

DAY 4

Coach and Rehearse

Paired Repeated Reading—Have students practice reading in small groups of four or five and individually for the group. While students are working, circulate and work with individual students, coaching them on reading with greater meaning and expression. For example, have the students read the poem emphasizing the first word in each line. After practice, ask a few students to perform the selection alone or in small groups.

Using the Audio CD—Students who are working together can go to the listening center to play the audio CD together and practice reading their parts. They can also record their reading of the selection and listen to it for self-evaluation.

Dress Rehearsal—Allow time for prepared students to present their readings before an audience of peers and teachers. Post a sign-up sheet for students who want to participate.

Build Skills and Strategies

Word Wall (see p. 99)—With the students, choose two to four interesting words from the poem to add to the Word Wall. Practice reading and spelling the words on the Word Wall daily.

Sentence Reading and Ordering—Write each line of the poem on a separate sentence strip then present each strip to students in random order. Read each strip (point to the words as they are read) and have them repeat it. Then display them on a bulletin board. Once all the strips are read, have students arrange the sentences into the original order.

Independent Work—Assign the *Word Work* activities on page 15 of the Student Book. These activities reinforce the letter *p* and the sound associated with it and may be completed at home or during another time. Before assigning this activity, conduct a mini-lesson on the letter *p* and how to write it.

DAY 5

Perform and Celebrate

Designate a time on Day 5 for students to invite special guests and perform their favorite selection. Create a special setting for the performances. The reading selections need not be those that students have worked on during the week, but those they feel comfortable with and can perform with appropriate volume, expression, and meaning. Students may want to prepare special artwork or props for the selection they choose to perform.

Word Work

Find the Letter

1. Circle the pictures whose names begin with the letter **p**. Write the letter **p** next to the pictures you circled.

Pancakes 15

Pancakes   29

Understanding the Fluency Development Lesson

The Fluency Development Lesson (FDL) is a fast-paced instructional routine for improving reading fluency, word recognition, and comprehension. Here are the steps in the FDL, which form a continuous cycle of daily focus on fluency.

About the Fluency Development Lesson

The *Reading Leadership Academy Guidebook* published by the U.S. Department of Education recently said:

"The FDL is a model of fluency instruction . . . that could be readily integrated into the regular reading curriculum (and employs) an extensive array of principles implemented over the course of a school year." It also states, *"The FDL experimental approach resulted in fluency gains for students, and teachers response was positive."*

DAY 1

Read Selection 1

The Fluency Development Lesson begins on Day 1 with an introduction to a new reading selection. The selection is then read aloud to students several times. After modeling, students begin to practice the selection in a variety of ways. Set aside 10 to 15 minutes for these activities.

Introduce and Discuss

Introduce

Begin the Fluency Development Lesson by providing background knowledge for the selection that you will be reading. This can be done by talking about the topic and nature of the text. Bring in an object or artifact related to the selection to share with students, such as sports memorabilia for a selection about a sporting event. The more background shared with students about the selection, the better they will comprehend its meaning. Also discuss the spelling, pronunciation, and meaning of some of the words students will encounter in the selection. This will assist in developing their vocabulary and focusing their attention on meaning.

Ask Questions

After building background, ask questions related to the topic, and elicit students' own questions about it. For example, after introducing and building background for a poem titled "Conversation," a poem about a conversation between a cat and a fish:

1. Ask students to speculate on the kind of conversation they might expect between the two animals.
2. Record the students' responses on the board or chart paper.

Evoke Moods and Feelings

Since one purpose of reading is to evoke feelings in the reader, ask students to share the moods or feelings they have about a particular topic. For example, before reading the poem, "Conversation," ask students if they have cats and/or fish for pets. Direct them to share their feelings about what it is like to have cats and fish as pets. Record some of their statements.

Model Read and Read Together

Model Read

Read the selection aloud two or three times to the students in the way you would like them to read it. Ask them to follow along silently and to listen closely to your reading. Read with good volume, pace, expression, and diction.

After reading the selection to students, talk about how you read it.

- Did the students enjoy your reading?
- What did they like about it?
- Did the students think you read at the right volume and pace and with good expression?
- What did the students think when you emphasized particular words in the text?

Read the selection again in different voices. Try reading it like a robot, in a very high or low pitch, as a nervous Nellie, in a very sad voice, or with great joy. Have students comment on these interpretations of your reading.

If the selection to be read is a song lyric, read it to students before singing it. If you feel uncomfortable singing the lyrics, play the CD version of the passage for your students. Alternate between reading and singing the lyrics, with the goal of keeping students' attention focused on the text.

Choral Reading

Once you have modeled the selection for your students, direct them to read it with you chorally a couple of times. Echo read it the first time with you reading the selection line by line or phrase by phrase and the students repeating each line. (Later, one or two students can lead the echo reading.) Next, read the selection together as a group once or twice. If the selection is a song lyric, alternate between reading the selection and singing the song.

Then divide students into groups for antiphonal (alternating) choral reading. Direct girls to read selected lines and boys to read others; the entire class will then join in for the final few lines. Or, divide the class by birthday, eye color, or in any other way to add some variety in their practice of the selection.

Have students work on prosody by reading in different voices, at different paces, with different volumes (whisper and loud voices), and by emphasizing particular words. Be sure to remind students to look at the words as they read the selection. Even though they may have a selection memorized, it is important that they look carefully at each word as they read it. Further instruction specific to each selection is provided in the Teacher's Notes.

About Guided Oral Reading

What kinds of practice develop fluency? The *Report of the National Reading Panel* says:

"*. . . several procedures for developing fluency have been evaluated during the past two decades. These procedures typically emphasize repeated reading or guided oral reading practice.*"

Prosody

The Teacher Notes for each reading selection contain suggestions for prosodic reading. *Prosody* refers to the melodic aspects of oral reading. When you encourage students to read with appropriate prosody, you are also encouraging and nurturing their comprehension of the selection. You are asking them to think critically about the meaning of the selection and express that meaning through their voices.

Here are ways to focus students' attention on the prosodic aspects of their reading during the Fluency Development Lesson:

Pace—Read a text at various speeds, and see what happens to meaning. Vary the speed of reading within a text by reading one part at a faster pace and another part a bit more slowly. Add extended pauses into the text at appropriate places for effect.

Intonation and Expression—These refer to the tonal quality of the reading. Where does the tone of your voice go up, and where does it go down? Where do you extend the pronunciation of a sound in a word? How do you use oral expression to signal meaning? Play with these elements as you read to students and have them do so, too, when they read to you.

Volume—Students love to adjust the volume of their voices to various texts. Some texts are best interpreted in a loud voice, others in a whispery voice. Explore with students how volume can make reading passages more engaging and meaningful for the reader and listener.

Practice

After modeling and reading the selection together, tell students they will begin practicing reading the selection alone, in pairs, or in small groups, and at home. If time allows, have students begin practicing in class. Then encourage students to rehearse the selection at home with their parents, family members, or friends. You'll find that many family members greatly enjoy reading with their child and can easily help their child learn to read short selections with meaning and expression.

Related Selection

If students are progressing well with the main reading selection, a related selection is provided in the Teacher's Notes for many lessons. It can be used to challenge more advanced students or to provide additional choice for others. The related selection correlates
to the main selection by topic, theme, or skill.

If time permits, reproduce the related selection on the board or on chart paper and go through the same routine. If appropriate, students can then choose which selection they would like to practice and perform. Option: assign the related selection to be practiced at home for performance on the following day or on Day 5.

> When you encourage students to read with appropriate prosody, you are also encouraging and nurturing their comprehension of the selection. Meaning is embedded not just in the words, but in the way the words are expressed by the human voice.

Rehearse Selection 1

On the second day of the routine, students rehearse and perform the selection with your guidance and build comprehension and word recognition skills. Set aside 10 to 15 minutes to complete this phase.

Coach and Rehearse

Coaching

Work with individual students, listening to them practice the selection and giving them positive feedback. Tell them what they are doing well with the reading.

- Focus on accuracy, expression, phrasing, pacing, and overall meaningful interpretation.
- Model read the text for the student you are working with.
- Invite students to join you in two or three oral readings before asking them to read it on their own. This helps ensure success.

Paired Repeated Reading

Have the class work with partners for five to ten minutes. One student reads the selection to his or her partner three times. The partner should listen, help, and provide positive remarks after each reading, such as, "You read with good expression," or "Your pace was good." Then the listening student reads the text to the partner several times.

Do this activity in groups of three or four for greater variety. Remember, the goal is to get as many readings as possible in the few minutes you have for coaching and rehearsal. Students can also practice the selections independently when you are coaching other students.

Using the Audio CD

Audiotaped readings that accompany the selections include two readings by two different voices. They provide yet another interpretation of the selection for students to consider and evaluate. The readings serve as oral reading role models that students can use repeatedly. Encourage students to listen to and read along with the recordings for additional modeling and reading practice. If your classroom has centers, consider making a listening center with the audio CD.

Direct pairs of students, especially those who are having difficulty with the text, to listen to the audio CD of the selection several times before practicing the selection on their own. They should follow along by reading silently.

Dress Rehearsal

The dress rehearsal is one last time for students to practice the selection. Students perform the selection before a small audience of peers or other adults. Remind them that this is only a practice session for the reading celebration on Day 5. Students read and perform either the main text or the related selection for the rehearsal. Additionally, students can choose to practice favorite selections and poems from previous weeks in their dress rehearsal.

Build Skills and Strategies

Comprehension and Word Study Activities

Although *Fluency First!* focuses mainly on the texts students practice and perform, quick activities (maximum of five minutes) will extend student's learning. Several options for short, game-like activities that will enhance children's phonemic and phonological awareness, decoding, vocabulary, and comprehension are recommended in the Teacher's Notes for each selection. Students will find these activities enjoyable and will be able to experience success with them. See pages 16–17 for a summary of skills and strategies covered and pages 94–105 in the Appendix for a detailed description of each activity. In addition, paper and pencil activities are included with each selection in the student book. These skill-building activities can be completed in class or at home.

About Repeated Oral Reading

What kinds of practice improve reading? The *Report of the National Reading Panel* says:

Classroom practices that encourage repeated oral reading with feedback and guidance [lead] to meaningful improvements in reading for students— for good readers as well as for those who are experiencing difficulty.

DAY 3

Read Selection 2

A new reading selection is introduced on the third day of the routine. Follow the same procedures as you did on Day 1 to introduce, discuss, model read, and read the selection together.

DAY 4

Rehearse Selection 2

On Day 4, repeat the same procedure as you did on Day 2 with the second selection. Coach students as they rehearse the selection and conduct appropriate skill-development activities in phonemic and phonological awareness, decoding, vocabulary, and comprehension.

> Reading fluency and word recognition will improve when students practice connecting the written form of the words with their oral representations.

DAY 5

Perform Selections 1 and 2

Designate a time on the fifth day for celebrating oral reading. The anticipation of this event throughout the week will keep students motivated and focused on developing their comprehension and fluency.

Perform and Celebrate

Prepare for the Performance

Prepare the room by clearing a space for students to perform.

- Set up a special chair or music stand to indicate the place for the performer(s) to sit or stand.
- Consider lowering the lights and having the students sit on the floor in front of the speaker.

When appropriate, invite a parent, the school principal, and others to attend your celebration. Students perform better when they know there is an authentic audience for their performance.

In addition to the selections practiced during the week, allow students to choose poems and texts they have read from previous weeks or new poems or texts they have found on their own. Be sure students can read them with appropriate volume, expression, and meaning. As students begin to value this weekly celebration, encourage them to look for selections on their own that they can perform for their audience.

Remember, memorization is not a goal in this program. Allow students to memorize the selection if they like, but encourage them to have the text in front of them when they perform. Reading fluency and word recognition will improve when students practice connecting the written form of the words with their oral representations.

Building Reading Skills and Strategies

This program gives students the opportunity to build reading skills and strategies. Included in the Teacher's Notes for each reading selection are suggestions for short, game-like activities that can enhance children's phonemic and phonological awareness, decoding, vocabulary, and comprehension. These skill- and strategy-building activities are described in detail in the Appendix. Take time to familiarize yourself with them. The activities are referenced throughout the Teacher Notes.

Activities to Promote Phonemic and Phonological Awareness

Phonological awareness is an awareness that oral speech can be divided into sentences and that within words are syllables, onsets, rimes, and phonemes. *Phonemic awareness* is the ability to notice, understand, blend, segment, and manipulate the individual sounds in spoken words. This is not the same as phonics, which focuses on sound-symbol relationships. Phonemic awareness focuses on how the sounds of spoken language work to make spoken words.

Many kindergarteners and some older students will benefit from phonemic and phonological awareness activities based on the texts. These activities vary in difficulty. They are listed below from easiest to most challenging:

Phonological Awareness

- Rhyming
- Alliteration: Recognizing words that begin with the same sound
- Onset/Rime: Recognizing words that end with the same word family
- Isolating beginning or ending sounds

Phonemic Awareness

- Blending sounds to make a word
- Segmenting words into constituent sounds
- Substituting a sound to make a new word

See pages 94–95 for phonemic and phonological awareness games to play with words found in the selections.

Activities to Promote Decoding and Vocabulary

Proficient reading requires students to become masters of words—how they are decoded (sounded), how they are spelled, and what they mean. Indeed, one aspect of reading fluency involves learning to decode words quickly, effortlessly, and automatically.

Fluency First! recognizes the importance of word study and has included opportunities for you to engage your students in enjoyable and effective word study activities. The activities involve students selecting the words they study, continual practice of words, word building, and word play. Done regularly, these activities will help your students develop a deep understanding of the words that make up our language.

Refer to pages 96–101 in the Appendix for a description of the word study activities.

About Skill Instruction

What kinds of practices develop reading skills? The *Report of the National Reading Panel* says:

Multiple strategy instruction that is flexible as to which strategies are used and when they are taught over the course of a reading session provides a natural basis for teachers and readers to interact over text.

Activities to Promote Comprehension

Fluency First! promotes fluency through expressive and meaningful reading of texts and through the development of automaticity in decoding so that students can devote their attention to making sense of what they read.

Additional comprehension building activities that you can use with the selections in *Fluency First!* are also included. These comprehension activities get students thinking deeply about the meaning of the selection through:

- prediction
- imagery
- discussion
- vocabulary
- writing

Refer to pages 102–105 in the Appendix for a description of these activities.

Assessing Student Progress in Fluency

Fluency First! includes several methods for assessing and tracking student progress in reading. At the kindergarten level, informal assessment and self-assessment are provided in the program. Formal assessment measures are introduced in first grade. These assessment tools can provide an accurate measure of student progress in comprehension, word recognition, and fluency.

Informal Assessment

Informal assessment shows how a child works with typical classroom tasks. You may want to conduct a purposeful observation of each of your students weekly or monthly. You can keep anecdotal notes or use one of the three informal assessment forms found in the Appendix on pages 106–109. Select the form that best fits your teaching style. They can be used interchangeably and are described below.

The Fluency Observation Chart

This chart found on page 106 can be duplicated and used throughout the year as well. You might want to carry a clipboard and observe selected children, especially during the Coach and Rehearse portion of the Fluency Development Lesson. You can make notes such as, "Mark varied the volume and tone of his voice at appropriate places in the selection" in the boxes on the chart.

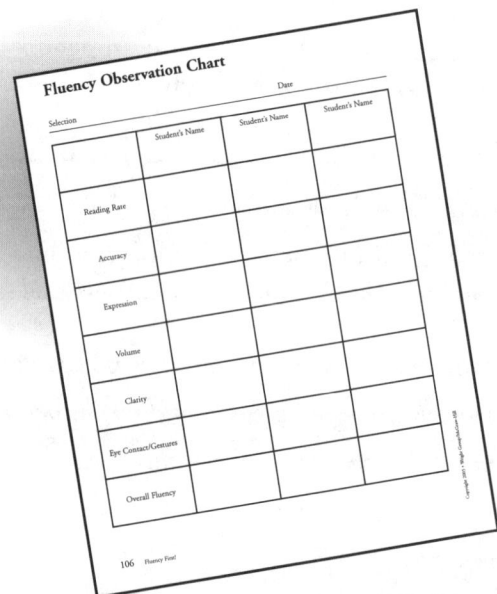

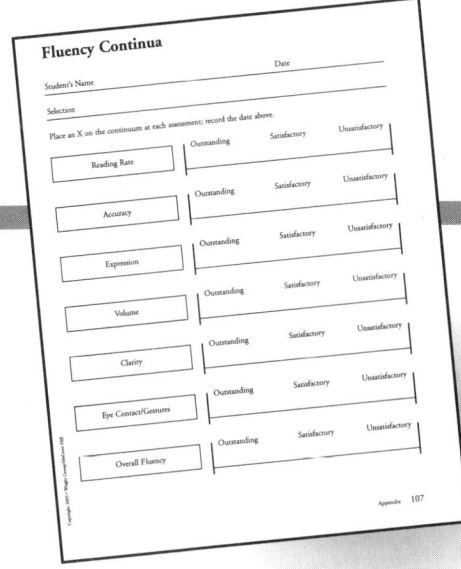

The Fluency Continua

This continua found on page 107 is a single sheet you can use all year to summarize your assessments of each student's fluency. Each time you mark the continua, add the date above the mark. This way you will see progress at a glance.

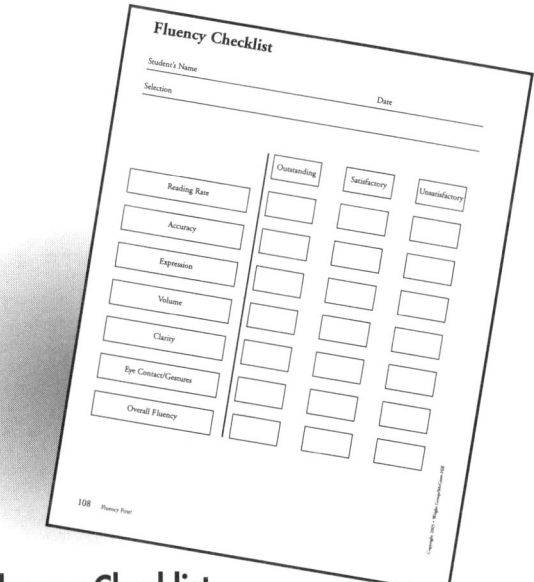

The Fluency Checklist

The checklist found on page 108 is another variation or way to capture the same information. Some teachers prefer checklists to continua or observation grids.

Aspects of Fluency

Each of these informal assessment forms is based on the same principles. You will consider several aspects of the child's fluency and evaluate their reading as outstanding, satisfactory, or unsatisfactory. The aspects of fluency to consider and assess are:

Reading Rate—Did the child read with appropriate speed and vary the reading rate as required?

Accuracy—This is a quick judgment of word recognition accuracy, although you may also want to consider whether the child read most words correctly the first time or frequently had to go back to correct mistakes, etc.

Expression—Did the child read with enthusiasm and express the feelings of the author? Did his or her voice change to express different moods or feelings in the selection?

Volume—Did the child read aloud at an appropriate volume?

Clarity—Was it easy or difficult to understand what the child was saying? Did the child articulate effectively and read at an appropriate pace?

Eye Contact/Gestures—This is the place to record performance features of the child's reading.

Overall Fluency—This is an overall assessment of the child's fluency. How does the student sound as a reader?

Many teachers keep completed informal assessment forms in children's reading portfolios or folders.

Self-Assessment

Students should also have some say in evaluating their own growth. Self-assessment benefits students because it helps them begin to take responsibility for their own learning.

Children can keep checklists or charts to assess their own reading. See page 109 in the Appendix for a reproducible checklist students can use for self-assessment. Help young students (K–1) complete the checklist by reading the items to them and facilitating response in a whole-group situation.

In addition, a quick assessment tool is provided for each selection in the Student Book. Students should mark their evaluation after performing each passage. Discuss these assessments with children occasionally

Children can also record insights in reading logs or reading journals. You can help them do this by posing fluency-related questions:

- Did I speak clearly?
- Did I speak loud enough?
- Did my reading sound like talk?
- How smooth was my reading today?
- Why do I think so (or how do I know)?

When you encourage students to evaluate their own reading, you will find that this practice has several benefits. Students learn to take control of their reading behavior and become more aware of their growth as readers, and you will have yet another source of information about your students.

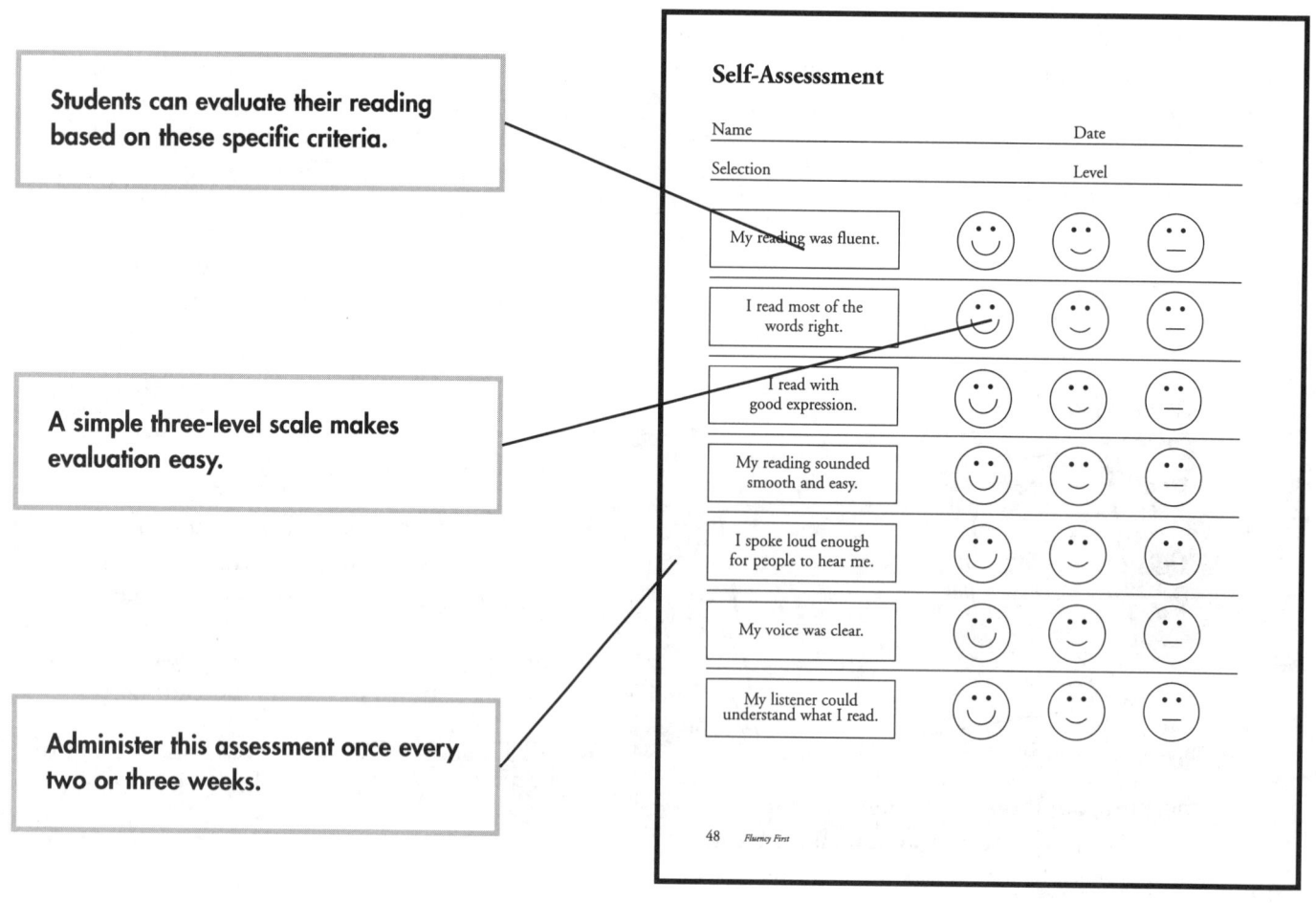

Students can evaluate their reading based on these specific criteria.

A simple three-level scale makes evaluation easy.

Administer this assessment once every two or three weeks.

Self-Assesssment

Name _____ Date _____

Selection _____ Level _____

| My reading was fluent. |
| I read most of the words right. |
| I read with good expression. |
| My reading sounded smooth and easy. |
| I spoke loud enough for people to hear me. |
| My voice was clear. |
| My listener could understand what I read. |

48   *Fluency First*

Teacher's Notes

Introduce the Fluency Development Lesson

Pages 22 through 93 of this guide provide detailed Teacher's Notes for implementing the Fluency Development Lesson (FDL) on a daily basis with each reading selection. Before introducing the first selection, take time to explain to students the FDL routine.

Introduce—Explain to students that each day they will practice becoming a fluent reader. Tell them that a fluent reader is one who reads each word correctly without hesitation. A fluent reader also reads to express the meaning of what is being read. Demonstrate fluent reading using the following sentence,

"I can't eat too many chicken wings."

First read the sentence accurately with an appropriate rate, but with little expression. Ask students what the sentence means. Next, read the sentence emphasizing the words *I can't eat*. Ask what the sentence now means (the person can eat a lot of wings). Next read the sentence emphasizing the words *too many*. Ask how this changed the meaning of the sentence (the person cannot eat many wings). Discuss with students how meaning can change with they way they express the reading.

Further explain that students will be reading and practicing at least two selections each week. At the end of the week, they will have an opportunity to perform one of the selections to the class and other invited guests.

Tell students they will repeat the following steps with each reading selection. Have them look at the pictures on pages 6 and 7 of their books as you explain the steps.

(1) **Listen**—Explain that you will read a selection aloud several times. Each time you will use a different voice so students can hear different ways it can be read. Then you will discuss which reading students liked best.

(2) **Read Along**—Next students will read along with you several times. Sometimes all students will read along. Other times groups of students will alternate reading certain pieces of the selection.

(3) **Practice in Class**—Step three is to practice reading the selection in small groups. Each student will read the selection at least three times, and fellow classmates will offer suggestions for improving the reading.

(4) **Practice at Home**—Explain that each night, students will take their book home and continue practicing reading the selection with a family member or friend.

(5) **Build Reading Skills**—Tell students that they will also be building their reading skills through activities in the book (point to a Word Work activity) and others that you provide. Sometimes, they will complete an activity at home.

(6) **Perform**—Finally, explain to students that at the end of each week, they will celebrate their hard work by performing one of the selections for the entire class. Further explain that sometimes you will invite special guests, such as other teachers, the principal, other classes, or their family to join in on the celebration.

Teacher's Notes—"Mary Had a Little Lamb"

DAY 1

Introduce and Discuss

"Mary Had a Little Lamb" is a familiar nursery rhyme that students will be able to recite with ease. Use this knowledge to help them read the words.

Introduce—Direct students to the selection on page 8, or display it using chart paper or a transparency. Tell students that they are going to read along as you read the words to a song they may know.

Ask Questions—Ask students what they would do if someone brought a lamb to school. Then hum the melody, and ask students if they have heard the song. Ask if students are familiar with the words to the song. If so, have them sing it.

Evoke Mood and Feeling—Ask students if they have ever petted a lamb at a petting zoo or a farm. Have them describe what lambs are like and how their fleece feels to the touch.

Model Read and Read Together

Prosody—Read the selection aloud several times using different voices. Point to the words as you read. Read the selection in a whisper, a singsong, or a dramatic voice. After each reading, ask students what they think about how you used your voice to express feelings.

Choral Reading—Move from modeling the poem to choral reading with students. Read the selection once echo style, then read and sing it together two or three times. Point to the words in the selection as you read it or sing it.

Practice—After modeling and reading the selection together, have students practice the selection alone, in pairs, or in small groups for a few minutes. Encourage students to rehearse the selection at home with family members and friends.

Related Reading—If students are progressing well, ask them if they know the rest of the rhyme. Read verses three and four to students.

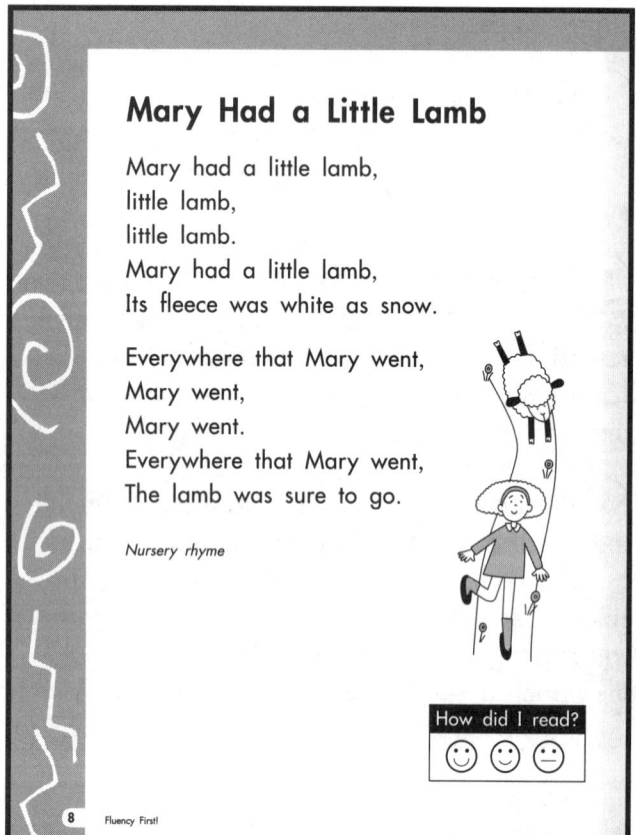

Mary Had a Little Lamb

Mary had a little lamb,
little lamb,
little lamb.
Mary had a little lamb,
Its fleece was white as snow.

Everywhere that Mary went,
Mary went,
Mary went.
Everywhere that Mary went,
The lamb was sure to go.

Nursery rhyme

How did I read?

8 Fluency First!

A Related Selection
Mary Had a Little Lamb (verses 3 & 4)

It followed her to school one day,
school one day,
school one day.
It followed her to school one day,
Which was against the rules.

It made the children laugh and play,
laugh and play,
laugh and play.
It made the children laugh and play,
To see a lamb at school.

Mother Goose

Coach and Rehearse

Paired Repeated Reading—Have students practice reading in small groups of four or five and individually for the group. Circulate and work with individual students, coaching them on reading with greater meaning and expression. Encourage students to practice different ways to emphasize the rhyming phrases: "white as snow" and "sure to go." After practice, ask a few students to perform the selection for the class alone or in small groups.

Using the Audio CD—Students who are working together can go to the listening center to play the audio CD together and practice reading their parts. They can also record their reading of the selection and listen to it for self-evaluation.

Dress Rehearsal—Allow time for prepared students to present their readings before an audience of peers and teachers. Post a sign-up sheet for students who want to participate.

Build Skills and Strategies

Print Awareness—Refer to the selection on chart paper. Ask students questions such as:
- How many words are in the first (or second, or last) line?
- Where is the word *lamb* (or *Mary*)?
- How many times is the word *lamb* (or *Mary*) in the poem?
- Where are capital *M*s? Where are lowercase *m*s?

Ask selected students to point at or circle the answers.

Syllable Clap—Clap the syllables as you read the poem. Begin this by reading slowly and clapping yourself. Then invite students to join you. Repeat several times.

Independent Work—Assign the *Word Work* activities on page 9 of the Student Book. These activities will reinforce word and letter recognition skills and may be completed at home or during another time.

Word Work

Picture Match

1. Draw a line to match each picture with a word. Trace the words.

snow

lamb

girl

Shape Search

2. Write two words from the poem that begin with **L**.

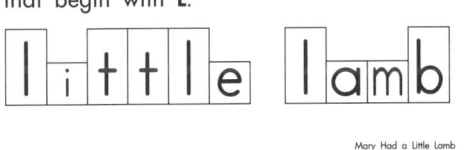

little lamb

Mary Had a Little Lamb   9

Teacher's Notes—"Ice Cream"

DAY 3

Introduce and Discuss

"Ice Cream" provides students with an opportunity to read antiphonally as well as chorally and individually.

Introduce—Direct students to the selection on page 10, or display it using chart paper or a transparency. Tell students that they are going to read along as you read a silly poem.

Ask Questions—Ask students to say, "I scream," first clearly speaking each word and then more quickly, running the words together. Ask them what dessert they hear when they say the words "I scream" quickly.

Evoke Mood and Feeling—Ask students what they feel when they hear the word *scream*. Ask what kind of voice would a person use when saying the word *scream*.

Model Read and Read Together

Prosody—Read the selection aloud several times. Point to the words as you read. Let your voice get louder at each line. Gesture to indicate meaning for the pronouns (e.g., point to yourself for *I*, to the students for *you*, and to all for *we*).

Choral Reading—Move from modeling the poem to choral reading with students. Divide the class into three groups. Have each group read one line and then the entire class can join in for the final line. Direct students to point to the words as they read.

Practice—In addition to reading alone or together, the students can try antiphonal reading: Student 1 reads line 1, student 2 reads line 2, and both students read lines 3 and 4 together. Encourage students to rehearse the selection at home with family members and friends.

Related Reading—If students are progressing well, introduce "Go to Bed, Tom." Ask them to think about similarities in how the two selections can be read, such as making each line louder.

Ice Cream

I scream,
You scream,
We all scream
For ice cream!

Nursery rhyme

How did I read?

10   Fluency First!

A Related Selection
Go to Bed, Tom

Go to bed, Tom.
Go to bed, Tom!
Tired or not, Tom,
Go to bed, Tom.

Nursery rhyme

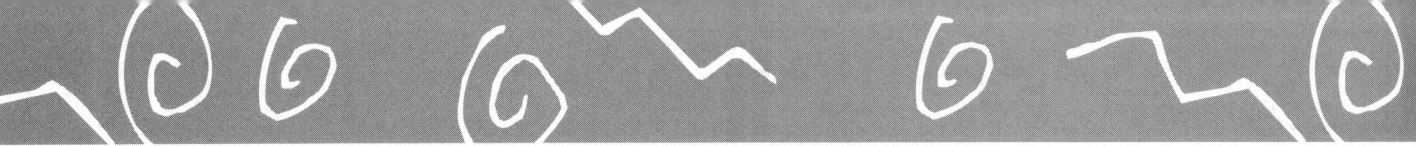

Coach and Rehearse

Paired Repeated Reading—Have students practice reading in small groups of four or five and individually for the group. Circulate and work with individual students, coaching them on reading with greater meaning and expression. Encourage students to voice the mood and feeling of the word *scream*. After practice, ask a few students to perform the selection they practiced for the class. They may perform alone or in small groups.

Using the Audio CD—Students who are working together can go to the listening center to play the audio CD together and practice reading their parts. They can also record their reading of the selection and listen to it for self-evaluation.

Dress Rehearsal—Allow time for prepared students to present their readings before an audience of peers and teachers. Post a sign-up sheet for students who want to participate.

Word Work

Picture the Words

1. Draw a picture to match each word.

I	we
Picture of one person	Picture of more than one person

Which is Which?

2. Draw a line to match the words and the pictures.

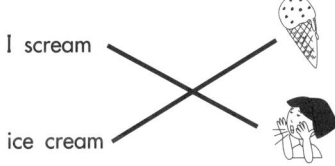

I scream

ice cream

Ice Cream **11**

Build Skills and Strategies

Word Ladder (see p. 100)—Guide students in creating new words derived from the word *ice* in the poem.

WORD	CLUE
ice	
mice	Add one letter to name a group of small animals with whiskers.
rice	Change the first letter to name something you eat.
nice	Change the first letter to describe a person who is good and friendly.
slice	Drop the first letter and add two to describe what you do with a knife.

Word Cards—Make word cards for the words in the poem. Ask students to find:
- words that have an *i*.
- words that identify people.
- words that have the /ē/ sound in them (say "*eeeeee*").

Independent Work—Assign the *Word Work* activities on page 11 of the Student Book. These activities will reinforce word recognition skills and may be completed at home or during another time.

Perform and Celebrate

Designate a time on Day 5 for students to invite special guests and perform their favorite selection. Create a special setting for the performances. The reading selections need not be those that students have worked on during the week, but those they feel comfortable with and can perform with appropriate volume, expression, and meaning. Students may want to prepare special artwork or props for the selection they choose to perform.

Teacher's Notes—"Hickory, Dickory, Dock"

Introduce and Discuss

"Hickory, Dickory, Dock" gives students an opportunity to practice fluent, rhythmic reading.

Introduce—Direct students to the selection on page 12, or display it using chart paper or a transparency. Tell students that they are going to read along as you read a nursery rhyme.

Ask Questions—Ask students to name the instrument that tells people the time. Show them a clock with hands or draw one on the board. Provide a brief explanation of how a clock works.

Evoke Mood and Feeling—Ask students to imagine the sounds at a clock shop, with clocks ticking, bells ringing on the hour, and cuckoo clocks with toy birds that chirp on the hour. Would they like being in the store?

Hickory, Dickory, Dock

Hickory, dickory, dock,
The mouse ran up the clock.
The clock struck one,
The mouse ran down!
Hickory, dickory, dock.

Nursery rhyme

How did I read?
☺ ☺ ☹

12 Fluency First!

Model Read and Read Together

Prosody—Read the selection several times. Point to the words as you read. Read it in staccato style, hesitating between words, to give the feeling of a clock.

Choral Reading—Move from modeling the poem to choral reading with students. Invite students to read the poem with you. Read it chorally several times, encouraging students to read it with louder and more expressive voices with each reading.

Practice—Divide the class into small groups and assign each group one line. Then perform the poem with each group reading their line. On subsequent readings, have groups change lines so that all lines are read by all students. Encourage students to rehearse the selection at home with family members and friends.

Related Reading—If students are progressing well, introduce "Hickory, Dickory, Dock II." As with the first poem, move from modeling the poem to choral reading with students. Ask students to compare the two poems and discuss how they are similar and different.

A Related Selection
Hickory, Dickory, Dock II

Hickory, dickory, dock
I only have one sock.
I have two feet,
and two shoes, too.
But I only have one sock.

Tim Rasinski

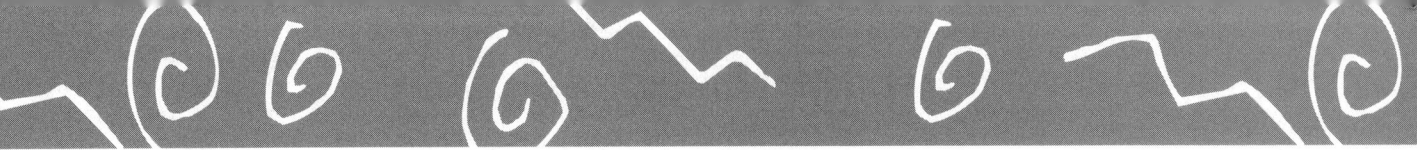

Coach and Rehearse

Build Skills and Strategies

Paired Repeated Reading—Have students practice reading in small groups of four or five and individually for the group. Circulate and work with individual students, coaching them on reading with greater meaning and expression. Suggest that they read "The mouse ran down!" especially fast to capture the surprise the mouse must have felt when the clock struck. After practice, ask a few students to perform the selection alone or in small groups.

Using the Audio CD—Students who are working together can go to the listening center to play the audio CD together and practice reading their parts. They can also record their reading of the selection and listen to it for self-evaluation.

Dress Rehearsal—Allow time for prepared students to present their readings before an audience of peers and teachers. Post a sign-up sheet for students who want to participate.

Word Wall (see p. 99)—With the students, choose two to four interesting words from the poem to add to the Word Wall. Practice reading and spelling the words on the Word Wall daily.

What's the Word (see p. 95)—Say some of the words from the poems that have two, three, or four sounds, one sound at a time (e.g., /d/, /o/, /k/ or /m/, /ow/, /s/). Have students say what the word is. Later, tell students individual words, and have them break each into its separate sounds.

Independent Work—Assign the *Word Work* activities on page 13 of the Student Book. These activities will reinforce beginning letters and sounds as well as the *-ock* word family. They can be completed at home or during another time.

Word Work

Name the Picture

1. Complete the word that names the picture. Trace the letters.

l
r
s

sock

lock

rock

Hickory, Dickory, Dock **13**

Teacher's Notes—"Pancakes"

DAY 3

Introduce and Discuss

"Pancakes" provides students an opportunity to practice fluent, rhythmic reading.

Introduce—Direct students to the selection on page 14, or display it using chart paper or a transparency. Take a show of hands of what students had for breakfast today (e.g., cereal, toast, eggs, bagel, fruit, pancakes). List the results of the poll on the board.

Ask Questions—Ask students to name the steps in frying an egg. Tell them that you are going to share a poem that describes how to make pancakes.

Evoke Mood and Feeling—Have students describe how they feel when they eat pancakes. Ask them to explain what pancakes taste like. Write the words on the board and read them to the students.

Model Read and Read Together

Prosody—Read the selection several times. Point to the words as you read. Emphasize the beginning word on each line. On subsequent readings accelerate your reading slightly as you move through the poem.

Choral Reading—Move from modeling the poem to choral reading with students. After three or four readings, invite students to read the poem with you. Read it chorally several times, encouraging students to read it with louder and more expressive voices with each reading. Soften your own voice as students develop mastery of the poem.

Practice—Divide the class into small groups and assign each group one line. Then perform the poem with each group reading their line. Encourage students to rehearse the selection at home with family members and friends.

Related Reading—If students are progressing well, introduce "More Pancakes." As with the first poem, move from modeling the poem to choral reading with students. Read it using the same expression used in the initial selection.

Pancakes

Mix the pancake,
Stir the pancake,
Pop it in the pan.
Fry the pancake,
Toss the pancake,
Catch it if you can.

Christina Rossetti

How did I read?
☺ ☺ ☹

14 Fluency First!

A Related Selection
More Pancakes

Butter the pancake,
Syrup the pancake,
Put it on your plate.
Smell the pancake,
Taste the pancake,
I'm sure I could eat eight!

Tim Rasinski

Coach and Rehearse

Build Skills and Strategies

Paired Repeated Reading—Have students practice reading in small groups of four or five and individually for the group. While students are working, circulate and work with individual students, coaching them on reading with greater meaning and expression. For example, have the students read the poem emphasizing the first word in each line. After practice, ask a few students to perform the selection alone or in small groups.

Using the Audio CD—Students who are working together can go to the listening center to play the audio CD together and practice reading their parts. They can also record their reading of the selection and listen to it for self-evaluation.

Dress Rehearsal—Allow time for prepared students to present their readings before an audience of peers and teachers. Post a sign-up sheet for students who want to participate.

Word Wall (see p. 99)—With the students, choose two to four interesting words from the poem to add to the Word Wall. Practice reading and spelling the words on the Word Wall daily.

Sentence Reading and Ordering—Write each line of the poem on a separate sentence strip then present each strip to students in random order. Read each strip (point to the words as they are read) and have them repeat it. Then display them on a bulletin board. Once all the strips are read, have students arrange the sentences into the original order.

Independent Work—Assign the *Word Work* activities on page 15 of the Student Book. These activities reinforce the letter *p* and the sound associated with it and may be completed at home or during another time. Before assigning this activity, conduct a mini-lesson on the letter *p* and how to write it.

Perform and Celebrate

Designate a time on Day 5 for students to invite special guests and perform their favorite selection. Create a special setting for the performances. The reading selections need not be those that students have worked on during the week, but those they feel comfortable with and can perform with appropriate volume, expression, and meaning. Students may want to prepare special artwork or props for the selection they choose to perform.

Word Work

Find the Letter

1. Circle the pictures whose names begin with the letter **p**. Write the letter **p** next to the pictures you circled.

Pancakes 15

Teacher's Notes—"Are You Sleeping?"

DAY 1

Introduce and Discuss

"Are You Sleeping?" provides an opportunity to read repeating phrases and to hear and read rhyming words.

Introduce—Direct students to the selection on page 16, or display it using chart paper or a transparency. Ask students how they wake up in the morning (e.g., alarm clock, mom calls, wake up on their own). List the choices on the board and tally the various responses. Tell students that today they will be reading a familiar song about sleeping.

Ask Questions—Ask them what time they go to bed and what time they wake up. How many enjoy sleeping in late in the morning?

Evoke Mood and Feeling—Ask students to pretend like they are sleeping. Then set off an alarm clock to wake them up from their "nap."

Model Read and Read Together

Prosody—Read the selection several times. Point to the words as you read. Alternate between reading and singing the song to students.

Choral Reading—Move from modeling the poem to choral reading with students. After two or three readings/singings, invite students to read and sing the poem with you. Have the girls read and sing the poem and then the boys. Give positive feedback to each group.

Practice—After reading the first song, have students listen to the recorded versions of the song while reading it on their own. Encourage students to rehearse the selection at home with family members and friends.

Related Reading—If students are progressing well, introduce "Where Has My Little Dog Gone." As with the first poem, move from modeling the poem to choral reading with students. Read and sing it several times to students using the same type of expression used in the main selection.

Are You Sleeping?

Are you sleeping,
Are you sleeping?
Brother John,
Brother John?
Morning bells are ringing,
Morning bells are ringing,
Ding ding dong,
Ding ding dong.

Traditional song

How did I read?

16 Fluency First!

A Related Selection
Where Has My Little Dog Gone

Oh where, oh where has my little dog gone?
Oh where, oh where can he be?
With his ears cut short and his tail cut long.
Oh where, oh where can he be?

Traditional song

Coach and Rehearse

Paired Repeated Reading—Have students practice reading in small groups of four or five and individually for the group. While students are working, circulate and work with individual students, coaching them on reading with greater meaning and expression. Encourage students to say the repeating lines with different intonation each time. After practice, ask a few students to perform the selection for the class alone or in small groups.

Using the Audio CD—Students who are working together can go to the listening center to play the audio CD together and practice reading their parts. They can also record their reading of the selection and listen to it for self-evaluation.

Dress Rehearsal—Allow time for prepared students to present their readings before an audience of peers and teachers. Post a sign-up sheet for students who want to participate.

Word Work

Name the Picture

1. Trace the word that names each picture.

 wing

 swing

 ringing

 swinging

Are You Sleeping? **17**

Build Skills and Strategies

Word Wall (see p. 99)—With the students, choose two to four interesting words from the poem to add to the class Word Wall. Practice reading and spelling these words daily.

Change the Word (see p. 95)—Ask students to change the beginning sounds of words from the poem. For example:
- My word is *bells*. Change the *b* to *y*. What is your word?
- Repeat changing *ding* to *dong*.

Independent Work—Assign the *Word Work* activities on page 17 of the Student Book. This activity will help students identify sounds and letters as well as the *-ing* word family. This activity can be completed at home or during another time.

DAY 3

Introduce and Discuss

"Spot" provides students an with opportunity to hear and read rhyming words.

Introduce—Direct students to the selection on page 18, or display it using chart paper or a transparency. Ask students to share the names of their dogs. If they don't have dogs, ask what they would name one if they did have one. List the names on the board, and read them.

Ask Questions—List on the board things that dogs like to do. Point out the sound–letter relationship as you write the words on the board. Read the words with your students.

Evoke Mood and Feeling—Ask students what kinds of dogs they like. Do they like big dogs or little dogs? Short-haired dogs or long-haired dogs? Playful dogs or lazy dogs?

Spot

I had a little pup,
   and his name was Spot.
Whenever we cooked,
   he licked the pot.
Whenever we ate,
   he never forgot
To lick the dishes
   as well as the pot.

Traditional rhyme

How did I read?
😊 😊 😐

18 Fluency First!

Model Read and Read Together

Prosody—Read the selection several times. Point to the words as you read. Emphasize the phrasing that helps make the poem so delightful to read. Read it slightly faster with each reading.

Choral Reading—Move from modeling the poem to choral reading with students. After three or four readings, invite students to read the poem chorally several times. Have students with blue eyes read it several times. Then have students with dark eyes read it. Give both groups praise and helpful feedback.

Practice—After reading and singing the poem, have students work in small groups or pairs to practice the poem. As students are practicing, roam the room and give positive feedback and coaching to students. Encourage students to rehearse the selection at home with family members and friends.

Related Reading—If students are progressing well, introduce "Wags." As with the first poem, move from modeling the poem to choral reading with students.

A Related Selection
Wags

My little puppy's name is Wags.
He eats so much his tummy sags.
His ears flip-flop and his tail wig-wags,
And when he walks, he makes zig-zags.

Tim Rasinski

Coach and Rehearse

Paired Repeated Reading—Have students practice reading in small groups of four or five and individually for the group. While students are working, circulate and work with individual students, coaching them on reading with greater meaning and expression. After practice, ask a few students to perform the selection they practiced for the class. They may perform alone or in small groups.

Using the Audio CD—Students who are working together can go to the listening center to play the audio CD together and practice reading their parts. They can also record their reading of the selection and listen to it for self-evaluation.

Dress Rehearsal—Allow time for prepared students to present their readings before an audience of peers and teachers. Post a sign-up sheet for students who want to participate.

Word Work

Picture Match

1. Draw a line to match each picture with a word. Write the word on the line.

lick   lick

dish   dish

pup   pup

pot   pot

Spot **19**

Build Skills and Strategies

Word Families—Write -ot on the board. Explain to students that it makes a certain sound and is called a word family because many words can be made with that same ending sound. Ask students to brainstorm words that belong to the -ot word family. Write the words on the board, and say them with the class. Go through the same procedure with the -ell and -ick word families.

Wordo (see pp. 100–101)—Provide students with a copy of the *Wordo* sheet and a set of markers. Have them randomly place the following words in each box: *little, pup, pot, spot, ate, forgot, dishes, pot,* and *name*. Then randomly call out the words and have students place a marker over any word that was called and is on their sheet. They win Wordo when they have three words covered in a row, a column, or a diagonal, or when they have covered the four corners.

Independent Work—Assign the *Word Work* activities on page 19 of the Student Book. These activities will reinforce word recognition skills and can be completed at home or during another time.

Perform and Celebrate

Designate a time on Day 5 for students to invite special guests and perform their favorite selection. Create a special setting for the performances. The reading selections need not be those that students have worked on during the week, but those they feel comfortable with and can perform with appropriate volume, expression, and meaning. Students may want to prepare special artwork or props for the selection they choose to perform.

Teacher's Notes—"Head, Shoulders, Knees and Toes"

DAY 1

Introduce and Discuss

"Head, Shoulders, Knees and Toes" is familiar and rhythmical and provides students an opportunity to work on fluent, rhythmical reading.

Introduce—Direct students to the selection on page 20, or display it using chart paper or a transparency. Tell students that they are going to read along as you read and sing a song they may be familiar with.

Ask Questions—Draw a large picture of a person on the board. Ask students: Where is the head? Where are the shoulders? Where are the knees? Where are the toes? Label the drawing as students offer answers.

Evoke Mood and Feeling—Have students point to various parts of their body that perform an action that you call out. For example, a mouth smiles, legs run, knees and elbows bend, etc.

Head, Shoulders, Knees and Toes

Head, shoulders, knees and toes,
    knees and toes

Head, shoulders, knees and toes,
    knees and toes

And eyes and ears and mouth
    and nose

Head, shoulders, knees and toes,
    knees and toes

Traditional rhyme

How did I read?

20   Fluency First!

Model Read and Read Together

Prosody—Read the selection several times. Point to the words as you read. Read it several ways, including reading it in a monotone voice like a robot. Ask students which version they like the best. Why? Discuss why it is important to read with good expression as well as speed.

Choral Reading—Move from modeling the poem to choral reading with students. Read it chorally several times, and have students point to their body parts that match each line of the story. Allow your own voice to soften as students develop mastery of the poem.

Practice—After modeling and reading the selection together, have students practice the selection in pairs or small groups for a few minutes. Encourage students to rehearse the selection at home with family members and friends.

Related Reading—If students are progressing well, introduce "If You're Happy and You Know It." Be sure students include hand claps and shouts where appropriate.

A Related Selection
If You're Happy and You Know It

If you're happy and you know it,
clap your hands
If you're happy and you know it,
clap your hands
If you're happy and you know it,
then your face will surely show it
If you're happy and you know it,
clap your hands.

Repeat the above substituting "stomp your feet," "shout Hurray!" and "do all three" for "clap your hands."

Traditional rhyme

Coach and Rehearse

Paired Repeated Reading—Have students practice reading in small groups of four or five and individually for the group. While students are working, circulate and work with individual students, coaching them on reading with greater meaning and expression. After practice, ask a few students to perform the selection they practiced for the class. They may perform alone or in small groups.

Using the Audio CD—Students who are working together can go to the listening center to play the audio CD together and practice reading their parts. They can also record their reading of the selection and listen to it for self-evaluation.

Dress Rehearsal—Allow time for prepared students to present their readings before an audience of peers and teachers. Post a sign-up sheet for students who want to participate.

Word Work

Label the Picture

1. Label the parts of the body.

| eye | head | knee | toe | nose |

Head, Shoulders, Knees and Toes **21**

Build Skills and Strategies

What's the Word (see p. 95)—Say some of the words from the poems that have two, three, or four sounds—one sound at a time (e.g., /t/, /ō/, /s/ or /h/, /e/, /d/). Have students say what the word is. Later, tell students individual words and have them break each into its separate sounds.

Wordo (see pp. 100–101)—Provide students with a copy of the *Wordo* sheet and a set of markers. Have them randomly place the following words in each box: *head, knees, toes, ears, mouth, eyes, nose,* and *and.* Have them color the center square and use it for a "free space." Then randomly call out the words and have students place a marker over any word that was called and is on their sheet. They win Wordo when they have three words covered in a row, a column, or a diagonal, or when they have covered all four corners.

Independent Work—Assign the *Word Work* activity on page 21 of the Student Book. This activity will introduce words that represent body parts and can be completed at home or during another time.

Teacher's Notes—"A Sailor Went to Sea"

DAY 3

Introduce and Discuss

"A Sailor Went to Sea" is both familiar and rhythmical. It provides students an opportunity to work on fluent, rhythmical reading.

Introduce—Direct students to the selection on page 22, or display it using chart paper or a transparency. Tell students that they are going to read along as you read a little poem that is a hand clapping game.

Ask Questions—Ask students if they know other hand clapping games to do alone or in pairs or groups. Invite a student or two to share.

Evoke Mood and Feeling—Ask students to think of words that describe the sea. Write the words on the board.

A Sailor Went to Sea

A sailor went to
    sea, sea, sea
To see what he could
    see, see, see
But all that he could
    see, see, see
Was the bottom of the deep blue
    sea, sea, sea.

Handclapping game

How did I read?

☺ ☺ ☹

Model Read and Read Together

Prosody—This poem is written with a singsong beat. Read and sing the selection aloud several times. Point to the words as you read. Increase the volume of your voice with each *see* or *sea*. Read it again, this time clapping your hands to keep track of the beat. Invite students to join you.

Choral Reading—Move from modeling the poem to choral reading with students. Ask students to wave their hands side to side to keep track of the beat. As a group, read and sing the poem several times.

Practice—After modeling and reading the selection together, have students practice the selection in pairs or small groups for a few minutes. Encourage students to rehearse the selection at home with family members and friends.

Related Reading—If students are progressing well, ask if they know another song about boats and streams. As with the first poem, move from modeling the poem to choral reading with students. Since many students will already know "Row, Row, Row Your Boat," invite students to sing and say the poem.

A Related Selection
Row, Row, Row Your Boat

Row, row, row your boat
Gently down the stream.
Merrily, merrily, merrily, merrily
Life is but a dream.

Traditional song

Coach and Rehearse

Paired Repeated Reading—Have students practice reading in small groups of four or five and individually for the group. While students are working, circulate and work with individual students, coaching them on reading with greater meaning and expression. You might challenge students to read this selection at an increasingly fast pace. After practice, ask a few students to perform the selection for the class alone or in small groups.

Using the Audio CD—Students who are working together can go to the listening center to play the audio CD together and practice reading their parts. They can also record their reading of the selection and listen to it for self-evaluation.

Dress Rehearsal—Allow time for prepared students to present their readings before an audience of peers and teachers. Post a sign-up sheet for students who want to participate.

Word Work

Picture This

1. Draw a picture of a sailor in a boat.

> Pictures will vary.

2. Draw a picture of the bottom of the sea.

> Pictures will vary.

A Sailor Went to Sea **23**

Build Skills and Strategies

Change the Word (see p. 95)—Ask students to change the beginning sounds of words from the poem. For example:
- My word is *see*. Change the *s* to *b*. What is your word?
- Repeat with *free*, *tree*, and *he*.
- Add the words to the Word Wall.

Clap the Poem—Show students how to clap for each syllable in the poem. Refer to the chart-sized version of the poem. To begin, read slowly. Point to each syllable as you read. Invite students to join you. Eventually, lower your own voice as students are able to read and clap, but continue pointing to syllables.

Independent Work—Assign the *Word Work* activities on page 23 of the Student Book. These activities will reinforce skills in understanding story content and can be completed at home or during another time.

Perform and Celebrate

Designate a time on Day 5 for students to invite special guests and perform their favorite selection. Create a special setting for the performances. The reading selections need not be those that students have worked on during the week, but those they feel comfortable with and can perform with appropriate volume, expression, and meaning. Students may want to prepare special artwork or props for the selection they choose to perform.

Teacher's Notes—"Husha"

Introduce and Discuss

"Husha" features the repetitive line "husha, husha, husha," which will allow you to read the poem in two-line stanzas. Students will be able to join you on the "husha" lines nearly immediately.

Introduce—Direct students to the selection on page 24, or display it using chart paper or a transparency. Tell students that they are going to read along as you read a song called a *lullaby*, which is a song used to lull or put a baby to sleep.

Ask Questions—Ask students if they know other lullabies. Ask them why we use lullabies and how someone's voice should sound when reading a lullaby.

Evoke Mood and Feeling—Ask students how to read the word "husha" so that it would help a baby go to sleep. Practice this with students, exaggerating the syllable break: "hushshshsh...a."

Husha

Husha husha husha
baby's sleeping

Husha husha husha
momma's leaping

Husha husha husha
daddy's sweeping

Husha husha husha
sister's creeping

Husha husha husha
brother's weeping

Husha husha husha
Sh sh sh

Sonja Dunn

How did I read?
☺ ☺ ☹

24 Fluency First!

Model Read and Read Together

Prosody—Read the selection aloud several times. Point to the words as you read. Decrease the volume of your voice with each "husha" line. At the second or third reading, invite students to join you.

Choral Reading—Move from modeling the poem to choral reading with students. Have half of the room read even lines and the other half read odd lines or all students read odd lines and individuals or pairs read even lines. Direct students to point to the words as they read.

Practice—After modeling and reading the selection together, have students practice the selection in pairs or small groups for a few minutes. Direct pairs to take turns with the lines (e.g., "Husha, husha, husha" for Student 1. "Baby's sleeping" for Student 2) and then trade lines. Encourage students to rehearse the selection at home with family members and friends.

Related Reading—If students are progressing well, introduce "Sh, Sh, Sh." As with the first poem, move from modeling the poem to choral reading with students. Explain that this is also a lullaby. Have students compare and contrast the different ways you read the lullaby.

A Related Selection
Sh, Sh, Sh

Out come the stars
Sh sh sh
Bright shines the
moon
Sh sh sh
Sweet sings nightbird
Sh sh sh

"Go to bed
Sleepyhead,"
Sandman said.
"Sh sh sh."

Sonja Dunn

Coach and Rehearse

Paired Repeated Reading—Have students practice reading in small groups of four or five and individually for the group. While students are working, circulate and work with individual students, coaching them on reading with greater meaning and expression. Encourage students to read with the kind of voice that would help babies go to sleep. After practice, ask a few students to perform the selection they practiced for the class. They may perform alone or in small groups.

Using the Audio CD—Students who are working together can go to the listening center to play the audio CD together and practice reading their parts. They can also record their reading of the selection and listen to it for self-evaluation.

Dress Rehearsal—Allow time for prepared students to present their readings before an audience of peers and teachers.

Word Work

Picture This

1. Draw a picture of baby sleeping.

   | Picture of baby sleeping. |

2. Draw a picture of daddy sweeping.

   | Picture of daddy sweeping. |

Husha **25**

Build Skills and Strategies

What's the Word? (see p. 95)—Tell students you will be saying individual sounds of a word from the poem. Say the sounds of the words slowly. Ask students to guess the words. Then invite students to add *-ing* and find the words on the chart-sized version of the poem.

- /s/, /l/, /ē/, /p/
- /l/, /ē/, /p/
- /sw/, /ē/, /p/
- /kr/, /ē/, /p/
- /w/, /ē/, /p/

Tableau (see p. 103)—Have individual students stand up in front of the class and perform a tableau. Each student should "freeze frame" their body to represent a line from the poem, such as "baby's sleeping" or "Momma's leaping." As the class guesses the part of the poem being depicted, encourage discussion of how each student interpreted the action.

Independent Work—Assign the *Word Work* activities on page 25 of the Student Book. These activities will reinforce comprehension and can be completed at home or during another time.

Teacher's Notes—"Tapping at the Window"

DAY 3

Introduce and Discuss

"Tapping at the Window" features a strong rhythm. Students may enjoy shouting the last line.

Introduce—Direct students to the selection on page 26, or display it using chart paper or a transparency. Tell students that they are going to read along as you read a little poem that is about someone tapping at the window and door.

Ask Questions—Ask students what they think tapping on a window sounds like. Write a few of their ideas on the board or chart paper.

Evoke Mood and Feeling—Ask students if they would be frightened or excited if they heard a tapping at their window. Ask them what kind of voices they would use to show that they were excited or frightened.

Model Read and Read Together

Prosody—Read the selection aloud several times. Point to the words as you read. For variety, read in an excited or frightened voice. Invite students to join you at the "1, 2, 3, 4!" line.

Choral Reading—Move from modeling the poem to choral reading with students. This selection lends itself to antiphonal reading. Have half of the room read lines 1 and 3 and the other half read lines 2 and 4. Then the whole class can read the last line together. Direct students to point to the words as they read.

Practice—After modeling and reading the selection together, have students practice the selection in pairs or small groups for a few minutes. Pairs could take turns with the lines and then trade lines. Encourage students to rehearse the selection at home with family members and friends.

Related Reading—If students are progressing well, introduce "Knocking on My Front Door." As with the first poem, move from modeling the poem to choral reading with students. Have students compare the similarities and differences between the poems. Ask if the sound of a knock is different from a tap.

Tapping at the Window

Tapping at the window,
Tapping at the door,
Everybody jumps up
When we count to four.
1, 2, 3, 4!

Counting rhyme

How did I read?
☺ ☺ ☹

A Related Selection
Knocking on My Front Door

Knocking on my front door.
Knocking at the back.
Just who might be coming?
It's my favorite Uncle Jack!

Tim Rasinski

Coach and Rehearse

Paired Repeated Reading—Have students practice reading in small groups of four or five and individually for the group. While students are working, circulate and work with individual students, coaching them on reading with greater meaning and expression. After practice, ask a few students to perform the selection they practiced for the class. They may perform alone or in small groups.

Using the Audio CD—Students who are working together can go to the listening center to play the audio CD together and practice reading their parts. They can also record their reading of the selection and listen to it for self-evaluation.

Dress Rehearsal—Allow time for prepared students to present their readings before an audience of peers and teachers. Post a sign-up sheet for students who want to participate.

Word Work

Words and Numbers

1. Write each numeral. Draw a picture for each.

| one | 1 | two | 2 |
| O | | O O | |

| three | 3 | four | 4 |
| O O O | | O O O O | |

Tapping at the Window **27**

Build Skills and Strategies

Presto-Chango (see p. 95)—Begin with the word *tap*. Then ask, "What do you get if you take the /t/ off of *tap*?" After students have identified the *-ap* word family, ask them to say words beginning with *m* (map), *l* (lap), /k/ (cap), *n* (nap), and *r* (rap). Add these words to the Word Wall.

Concepts about Print—Using the chart-sized version of the poem, ask students a variety of questions about words and letters, such as the ones below. Invite individual students to point to (or underline or circle) the print to show the answer.
- Which line is the same as the title?
- Where are two words that are the same?
- Which words begin with the letter *t*?
- Find the word *window.*
- Find the word *door.*

Independent Work—Assign the *Word Work* activities on page 27 of the Student Book. These activities will reinforce word recognition skills and number sense and can be completed at home or during another time.

Perform and Celebrate

Designate a time on Day 5 for students to invite special guests and perform their favorite selection. Create a special setting for the performances. The reading selections need not be those that students have worked on during the week, but those they feel comfortable with and can perform with appropriate volume, expression, and meaning. Students may want to prepare special artwork or props for the selection they choose to perform.

Teacher's Notes—"This Little Pig Went to Market"

DAY 1

Introduce and Discuss

"This Little Pig Went to Market" allows students to practice a familiar poem, learn words that are used repetitively, and read with expression.

Introduce—Direct students to the selection on page 28, or display it using chart paper or a transparency. Tell students that they are going to read along as you read a poem about pigs.

Ask Questions—Ask students what kinds of sounds different animals make. Have them give examples such as "baa" for sheep, "arf" for dogs, "meow" for cats, "moo" for cows, etc.

Evoke Mood and Feeling—Have students describe how they first heard this poem. Who taught it to them? Have they ever played this game with a younger child? Did the child like it?

This Little Pig Went to Market

This little pig went to market.
This little pig stayed at home.
And this little pig had roast beef.
And this little pig had none.
This little pig said, "Wee, wee, wee!
I can't find my way home."

Mother Goose

How did I read?

☺ ☺ ☺

28   Fluency First!

Model Read and Read Together

Prosody—Read the selection aloud several times using different voices for each pig. Point to the words as you read. After each reading, ask students what they think about the way you used your voice.

Choral Reading—Move from modeling the poem to choral reading with students. Divide the class into five groups. Have them read the poem aloud, with each group taking the part of one of the pigs. Direct students to point to the words as they read.

Practice—After modeling and reading the selection together, have students practice the selection alone, in pairs, or in small groups. Then encourage students to rehearse the selection by reading it aloud at home with family members.

Related Reading—If students are progressing well, introduce "Where Is Thumbkin?" Have them use the hand motions while they say it. Ask students to describe ways the poems are similar. Point out that both are accompanied by motions of the fingers or toes.

A Related Selection
Where Is Thumbkin?

Where is thumbkin? Where is thumbkin?

(refrain)
Here I am. Here I am.
How are you this morning? Very well, I thank you.
Run away. Run away.

Where is pointer? Where is pointer? (refrain)
Where is tall man? Where is tall man? (refrain)
Where is ring man? Where is ring man? (refrain)
Where is pinkie? Where is pinkie? (refrain)

Traditional song

Coach and Rehearse

Paired Repeated Reading—Have students practice reading in small groups of four or five and individually for the group. While students are working, circulate and work with individual students, coaching them on reading with greater meaning and expression. Encourage them to express each pig's personality with their voices. After practice, ask a few students to perform the selection they practiced for the class. They may perform alone or in small groups.

Using the Audio CD—Students who are working together can go to the listening center to play the audio CD together and practice reading their parts. They can also record their reading of the selection and listen to it for self-evaluation.

Dress Rehearsal—Allow time for prepared students to present their readings before an audience of peers and teachers.

Word Work

Picture Match

1. Draw a line to match each word with a picture.

home

pig

market

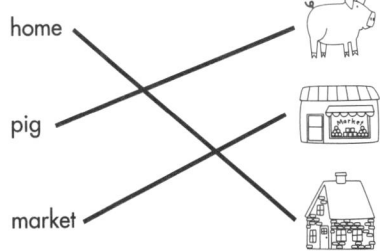

Shape Search

2. Write a word from the poem that begins with l.

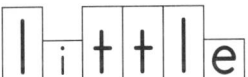

This Little Pig Went to Market **29**

Build Skills and Strategies

Sketch to Stretch (see p. 103)—Give students a minute or two to sketch the actions of one of the pigs in the poem. Ask them to form small groups to share their sketches and discuss how each sketch is related to the text.

Word Ladder (see p. 100)—Guide students in creating new words derived from the word *pig* in the poem.

WORD	CLUE
pig	
big	Change the first letter to describe something that is not small.
wig	Change the first letter to name hair that you wear as a costume.
dig	Change the first letter to name what you do to make a hole in the ground.
jig	Change the first letter to name a dance.

Independent Work—Assign the *Word Work* activities on page 29 of the Student Book. These activities will help students connect word spelling and meaning and can be completed at home or during another time.

This Little Pig Went to Market   43

Teacher's Notes—"Lunchtime"

DAY 3

Introduce and Discuss

"Lunchtime" gives students the chance to read and analyze a poem in ways that express different emotions about its subject.

Introduce—Direct students to the selection on page 30, or display it using chart paper or a transparency. Tell students that they are going to read along as you read a poem about an important part of the school day.

Ask Questions—Ask students what part of the day they enjoy the most. Ask for a show of hands of students who like lunchtime the best. Tell them that many people enjoy lunchtime, which is the subject of the poem they are about to read.

Evoke Mood and Feeling—Have students suggest different healthy things they like to eat for lunch. Record their suggestions on the board. Emphasize the importance of healthy food choices.

Lunchtime

Lunchtime, lunchtime
   never too soon.

My fork is ready
   and so is my spoon.

Ten 'til twelve,
   it's almost noon.

Lunchtime, lunchtime
   never too soon!

Tim Rasinski

How did I read?
☺ ☺ ☹

30   Fluency First!

Model Read and Read Together

Prosody—Read the poem aloud several times. Point to the words as you read. Express with your reading the different attitudes the speaker might have about lunchtime. Maybe the speaker feels so excited about lunchtime that he can barely contain himself. To express this attitude, read with a fast pace, elevated intonation, and louder volume. Or, the speaker may be feeling that lunchtime will never arrive. After each different reading, ask students how they think the speaker felt about lunchtime.

Choral Reading—Move from modeling the poem to choral reading with students. Read the poem once echo style, then read it together two or three times. Point to the words in the selection as you read it.

Practice—Have students practice the selection alone, in pairs, or in small groups for a few minutes. Have them act out the poem or invent motions for specific words and phrases. Encourage students to rehearse the selection at home with family members and friends.

Related Reading—If students are progressing well, introduce "Pizza Pie." Ask students to describe ways the poems are similar. Point out that both are about eating lunch. "Lunchtime" takes place just before lunch and "Pizza Pie" takes place just after lunch.

A Related Selection
Pizza Pie

Bite, chew, crunch and munch,
Pizza pie is great for lunch.
Top it off with fruity punch.
Oh my gosh I ate a bunch.

Tim Rasinski

Coach and Rehearse

Paired Repeated Reading—Have students practice reading in small groups of four or five and individually for the group. While students are working, circulate and work with individual students, coaching them on reading with greater meaning and expression. Help students figure out how to express the excitement and anticipation of lunch to a hungry person. After practice, ask a few students to perform the selection alone or in small groups.

Using the Audio CD—Students who are working together can go to the listening center to play the audio CD together and practice reading their parts. They can also record their reading of the selection and listen to it for self-evaluation.

Dress Rehearsal—Allow time for prepared students to present their readings before an audience of peers and teachers.

Word Work

Words and Pictures

1. Circle the picture that matches the word.

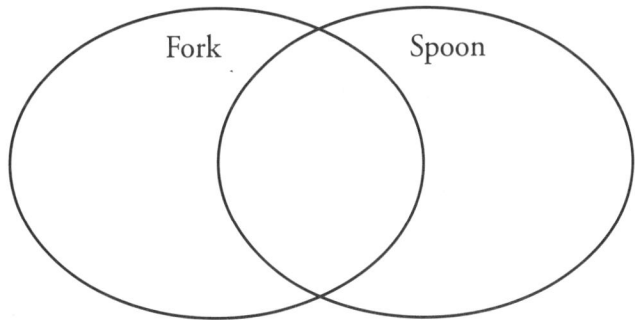

fork

spoon

ten

Words with oo

2. Write a word from the poem that matches each picture.

spoon   noon

Build Skills and Strategies

I Say (see p. 95)—Say a word from the poem. Have students say another word that rhymes. For example, say:

- I say *so*. You say ___.
- I say *too*. You say ___.
- Repeat with several other words.

Compare and Contrast (see p. 104)—Draw a Venn diagram. Label one side *Fork* and the other *Spoon*. Have students help you fill in the diagram with foods eaten with these utensils. Those that can be eaten with either utensil go in the center section.

Fork   Spoon

Independent Work—Assign the *Word Work* activities on page 31 of the Student Book. These activities will help students connect words and meanings and can be completed at home or during another time.

Perform and Celebrate

Designate a time on Day 5 for students to invite special guests and perform their favorite selection. Create a special setting for the performances. The reading selections need not be those that students have worked on during the week, but those they feel comfortable with and can perform with appropriate volume, expression, and meaning. Students may want to prepare special artwork or props for the selection they choose to perform.

Teacher's Notes—"The Itsy Bitsy Spider"

DAY 1

Introduce and Discuss

"The Itsy Bitsy Spider" provides students with the opportunity to sing and perform matching motions to a well-known song.

Introduce—Direct students to the selection on page 32, or display it using chart paper or a transparency. Show students a picture of a spider, or draw one yourself. Ask for a show of hands of students who think spiders are scary.

Ask Questions—Ask if the students know this song. If so, ask them to demonstrate the hand motions for this song. If not, demonstrate the motions for them. Have students discuss these motions. Do they fit the song?

Evoke Mood and Feeling—Ask students to suggest words and phrases that describe their feelings about spiders. Record these responses.

The Itsy Bitsy Spider

The itsy bitsy spider
Climbed up the water spout;

Down came the rain
And washed the spider out;

Out came the sun
And dried up all the rain;

And the itsy bitsy spider
Climbed up the spout again.

Traditional song

How did I read? ☺ ☺ ☺

32 Fluency First!

Model Read and Read Together

Prosody—Read the selection aloud several times, at first without the melody or motions. Vary your pace and intonation. Point out that a faster pace adds excitement to the song's narrative, while a slow pace shows a tough climb for the spider. Point to the words as you read.

Choral Reading—Move from modeling the poem to choral reading with students. Read the poem as a group. Then divide the class into two groups. Have one group read the lines aloud leaving out the direction words *up*, *down*, and *out*. The second group can supply the direction words.

Practice—After modeling and reading the selection together, have students practice either or both the selections alone, in pairs, or in small groups for a few minutes. Encourage students to rehearse the selection at home with family members and friends.

Related Reading—If students are progressing well, introduce "Little Miss Muffet." Explain the words *tuffet* (a stool), *curds* (thick part of sour milk), and *whey* (watery part of sour milk). Then ask students to compare the roles of the spider in each selection. Ask students to make up motions for the second selection and explain the motions they suggest.

A Related Selection
Little Miss Muffet

Little Miss Muffet
Sat on a tuffet,
Eating her curds and whey.
Along came a spider,
Who sat down beside her,
And frightened Miss Muffet away.

Nursery rhyme

Coach and Rehearse

Paired Repeated Reading—Have students practice reading in small groups of four or five and individually for the group. While students are working, circulate and work with individual students, coaching them on reading with greater meaning and expression. Have students use their voices to express the ideas of "up" and "down." After practice, ask a few students to perform the selection for the class alone or in small groups.

Using the Audio CD—Students who are working together can go to the listening center to play the audio CD together and practice reading their parts. They can also record their reading of the selection and listen to it for self-evaluation.

Dress Rehearsal—Allow time for prepared students to present their readings before an audience of peers and teachers. Post a sign-up sheet for students who want to participate.

Word Work

Shape Search

1. Write two words from the poem that begin with **sp**.

s	p	o	u	t

s	p	i	d	e	r

2. Write a word from the poem that begins with **r**.

r	a	i	n

Same Meaning

3. Write the words from the poem that mean **teeny-weeny**.

   itsy   bitsy

   The Itsy Bitsy Spider **33**

Build Skills and Strategies

Change the Word (see p. 95)—Say the word *all* from the selection. Ask questions like:
- What word do you get when you add *b* to *all*?
- When you add *c*?
- When you add *f*?
- When you add *m*?
- When you add *t*?
- When you add *w*?

Sketch to Stretch (see p. 103)—Give students a few minutes to sketch something related to one of the two texts such as:
- the itsy bitsy spider climbing up the water spout.
- the spider being washed down.
- Little Miss Muffet being frightened by the spider.

Have students form groups of three and share their sketches. Ask the groups to discuss how each sketch is related to the text.

Independent Work—Assign the *Word Work* activities on page 33 of the Student Book. These activities will reinforce letter recognition and vocabulary and can be completed at home or during another time.

Teacher's Notes—"Red Means Stop"

Introduce and Discuss

"Red Means Stop" gives students the opportunity to examine images and learn sounds and words through repetition.

Introduce—Direct students to the selection on page 34, or display it using chart paper or a transparency. Tell students to think about the colors in a traffic light: red, yellow, and green.

Ask Questions—Ask students to describe a traffic light and the meanings of the different colors.

Evoke Mood and Feeling—Ask students how they feel when they cross a busy street. What do they do to cross safely?

Red Means Stop

Stop! Stop! Do not go.
The big red sign tells us so.
I know that,
and so does Joe.
Red means stop,
and green means go.

Tim Rasinski

How did I read?

34 Fluency First!

Model Read and Read Together

Prosody—Read the selection aloud several times using different voices, paces, and intonations. Point to the words as you read. Then leave out the word *go* in the first and last lines and *stop* in the fifth line. Ask students to fill in the missing words from memory as you read the selection again.

Choral Reading—Move from modeling the poem to choral reading with students. Direct students to point to each word in the selection as they read it. Divide the class into two groups. Have them read the poem aloud, alternating lines.

Practice—After modeling and reading the selection together, have students practice the selection in pairs. Then tell the students to rehearse the selection at home with family members and friends.

Related Reading—If students are progressing well, introduce "Hard at Work." Read the poem, drawing attention to the words *digger* and *worker*. Say, "A digger digs" and "A worker works." Ask students to supply similar sentences using jobs they know. Write out each suggestion. Explain that the letters *-er* at the end of a word mean someone who does the action the word describes.

A Related Selection
Hard at Work

Diggers and cranes
Diggers and cranes
The workers work hard
but they rest when it rains

Sonja Dunn

Coach and Rehearse

Paired Repeated Reading—Have students practice reading in small groups of four or five and individually for the group. Circulate and work with individual students, coaching them on reading with greater meaning and expression. Have students experiment reading the third and fourth line of the poem in a whisper, as if they are telling the audience a secret. After practice, ask a few students to perform alone or in small groups.

Using the Audio CD—Students who are working together can go to the listening center to play the audio CD together and practice reading their parts. They can also record their reading of the selection and listen to it for self-evaluation.

Dress Rehearsal—Allow time for prepared students to present their readings before an audience of peers and teachers. Post a sign-up sheet for students who want to participate.

Word Work

Words and Pictures

1. Write the word from the poem that goes on this sign.

Silent Letters

2. Circle the word that does not rhyme.

know   Joe   (stop)   so

Red Means Stop   **35**

Build Skills and Strategies

New Beginnings—Point out to students the /ō/ sound in the words *go, so, know,* and *Joe.* Ask them to help you list other words that have different beginning sounds but that end in the /ō/ sound. Suggestions include *bow, crow, dough, flow, hoe, low, mow, row slow, sew, so, toe, tow,* and *yo.*

Opposites—Play a riddle game with students to find opposites. Point out that *stop* and *go* are opposites. Then create riddles such as the following for students to answer:
- I am the opposite of *down,* and I rhyme with *cup.* (*up*)
- I am the opposite of *fast,* and I rhyme with *blow.* (*slow*)

Other opposites to use include *in–out, high–low, here–there, short–tall,* and *big–little.* Write a few of these on cards and add them to the Word Wall. Practice reading and spelling the Word Wall words daily.

Independent Work—Assign the *Word Work* activities on page 35 of the Student Book. These activities will reinforce rhyming and word recognition and can be completed at home or during another time.

Perform and Celebrate

Designate a time on Day 5 for students to invite special guests and perform their favorite selection. Create a special setting for the performances. The reading selections need not be those that students have worked on during the week, but those they feel comfortable with and can perform with appropriate volume, expression, and meaning. Students may want to prepare special artwork or props for the selection they choose to perform.

Teacher's Notes—"Shoes"

Introduce and Discuss

"Shoes" provides students with an opportunity to hear and use repetitive phrases and to read using a singsong voice.

Introduce—Direct students to the selection on page 36, or display it using chart paper or a transparency. Tell students that they will read along as you read a poem. Point out the word *pullover* and ask if anyone is wearing shoes with pullover straps. How do they work?

Ask Questions—Ask students what are some words that tell about their shoes? (Examples: *sneakers, lace-up shoes, red, blue, white, dirty, old, new, untied*)

Evoke Mood and Feeling—Ask students if they have (or had) a favorite pair of shoes. Invite volunteers to describe their favorite pair of shoes. What makes (or made) those shoes special?

Shoes

White shoes, blue shoes,
old shoes, new shoes.
　　Lace'em up shoes,
　　Pullover strap shoes.

Dress shoes, play shoes,
night shoes, day shoes.
　　Lace'em up shoes,
　　Pullover strap shoes.

Laura Portalupi

How did I read?
☺ ☺ ☹

36　Fluency First!

Model Read and Read Together

Prosody—Read the poem several times in a singsong voice. Point to the words as you read. Read the poem in different ways, then ask students which way they liked best.

Choral Reading—Move from modeling the poem to choral reading with students. Organize three groups. Have the first group read the first line of each stanza, the second group read the second line, and the third group read the third and fourth lines. Read the poem two or three times, using singsong voices. Direct students to point to each word as they read it or hear it read.

Practice—After modeling and reading the selection together, have students practice either or both selections alone, in pairs, or in small groups. Then encourage students to rehearse the selection by reading it aloud at home with family members.

Related Reading—If students are progressing well, introduce "Grapefruit." Ask how both poems are the same. (They both repeat words.) Brainstorm with the class other word combinations that rhyme with *grapefruit*, such as *late–fruit, gate–fruit, cape–fruit,* and *shape–fruit.*

A Related Selection
Grapefruit

Grapefruit, grapefruit
sitting on my plate-fruit.
Grapefruit, grapefruit,
I can't wait-fruit.

Grapefruit, grapefruit.
pink or white-fruit.
Grapefruit, grapefruit,
mmm tastes great-fruit.

Laura Portalupi

Coach and Rehearse

Paired Repeated Reading—Have students practice reading in small groups of four or five and individually for the group. Circulate and work with individual students, coaching them on reading with greater meaning and expression. For example, they might use their voices and facial expressions to indicate which kinds of shoes they like and dislike. After practice, ask a few students to perform the selection they practiced for the class. They may perform alone or in small groups.

Using the Audio CD—Students who are working together can go to the listening center to play the audio CD together and practice reading their parts. They can also record their reading of the selection and listen to it for self-evaluation.

Dress Rehearsal—Allow time for prepared students to present their readings before an audience of peers and teachers.

Word Work

Picture Match

1. Draw a line from each picture to its name. Trace the words.

play shoes

dress shoes

Rhyming Words

2. Write two words from the poem that rhyme.

| p | l | a | y |

| d | a | y |

Shoes **37**

Build Skills and Strategies

Open Word Sort (see p. 98)—Have students brainstorm words that begin with /sh/ (e.g., *shirt, ship, shine, shark, shadow, sharp, shake, shade, short, shut*). Ask them to help you spell the words so you can write them on the board. Then have students sort the words in ways that make sense to them. They might begin by finding two words that are the same in some way, such as *shark* and *sharp* (both have the /ar/ sound). They might also look for words with the same vowel, for two-syllable words, or for words with similar meanings, such as *shadow* and *shade*.

What's the Word? (see p. 95)—Choose a word with /sh/ from the board (or a word from the selection) and say it slowly, pausing between sounds. Have students blend the sounds together and say the word. For example, you might say, "I'm thinking of what the sun does. Here are the sounds: /sh/, /ī/, /n/. What's the word?"

Independent Work—Assign the *Word Work* activities on page 37 of the Student Book. These activities will reinforce rhyming and word recognition skills and can be completed at home or during another time.

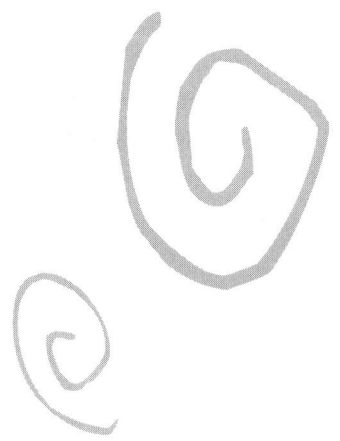

Teacher's Notes—"Drum"

Introduce and Discuss

"Drum" provides students with an opportunity to read a poem with many possibilities for rhythmic interpretation.

Introduce—Direct students to the selection on page 38, or display it using chart paper or a transparency. Tell students that they will read along as you read a poem. Explain that it includes sounds that are not words. Ask them to figure out why these sounds are in the poem.

Ask Questions—Have students name musical instruments. Do they know how to play any instruments? Does someone they know play an instrument? Which one? How is it played? What kinds of sounds does it make?

Evoke Mood and Feeling—Ask students what kind of music they like. How do they feel when they listen to their favorite music?

Drum

Ta ta ta ta,
ti ti ti,
tu tu,
ta ta, toe

Rump-pump,
bump-pump,
ree-tee tee

This is how my little drum
makes music just for me.

Sarah Hutt

How did I read?

Model Read and Read Together

Prosody—Read the poem several times, moving one hand as if you are playing a drum. With your other hand, point to each word or sound.

Choral Reading—Move from modeling the poem to choral reading with students. Organize the class into three groups. Have each group read a stanza. After the groups read the poem twice, have them switch stanzas. Have students point to each word in the selection as they read it or hear it.

Practice—After modeling and reading the selection together, have students practice one or both selections alone, in pairs or in small groups. Then encourage students to rehearse the selection by reading it aloud at home with family members.

Related Reading—If students are progressing well, introduce "Ten Tom-Toms." Ask how both poems are similar. (They are about drumming and have many short words that sound like drum beats.) Brainstorm with the class other words that sound like drum beats, such as *pop, top, dum, rum.*

A Related Selection
Ten Tom-Toms

Ten tom-toms,
Timpani, too,
Ten tall tubas
And an old kazoo

Ten trombones—
Give them a hand!
The sitting-standing-marching-running
Big Brass Band

Author unknown

Coach and Rehearse

Paired Repeated Reading—Have students practice reading in small groups of four or five and individually for the group. While students are working, circulate and work with individual students, coaching them on reading with greater meaning and expression. Tell students to try to make their voices sound like drum beats. After practice, ask a few students to perform the selection they practiced for the class. They may perform alone or in small groups.

Using the Audio CD—Students who are working together can go to the listening center to play the audio CD together and practice reading their parts. They can also record their reading of the selection and listen to it for self-evaluation.

Dress Rehearsal—Allow time for prepared students to present their readings before an audience of peers and teachers.

Word Work

Rhyming Words

1. Circle the picture whose name rhymes with **bump**.

jump   catch

2. Look at the word under the picture you circled. Write the word here.

Drum **39**

Build Skills and Strategies

Word Ladder (see p. 100)—Guide students in creating new words derived from the word *pump* in the poem.

WORD	CLUE
pump	
pup	Take away one letter to name a baby dog.
put	Change the last letter to make a word that means "to place something."
pet	Change the vowel to name a cat or dog.

Open Word Sort (see p. 98)—Point out that many words and sounds in the selection begin with /t/. Have students brainstorm other words that begin with /t/ (e.g., *time, turtle, table, tell, take, talk, taste, tape, teach, ten, test, teeth*). Ask them to help you spell the words so you can write them on the board. Then have students sort the words in ways that make sense to them, such as things (nouns), action words (verbs), and describing words (adjectives).

Independent Work—Assign the *Word Work* activities on page 39 of the Student Book. These activities will reinforce rhyming and word recognition skills and can be completed at home or during another time.

Perform and Celebrate

Designate a time on Day 5 for students to invite special guests and perform their favorite selection. Create a special setting for the performances. The reading selections need not be those that students have worked on during the week, but those they feel comfortable with and can perform with appropriate volume, expression, and meaning. Students may want to prepare special artwork or props for the selection they choose to perform.

Teacher's Notes—"Letters"

Introduce and Discuss

"Letters" familiarizes students with the letters of the alphabet and the initial position of a letter in a word.

Introduce—Direct students to the selection on page 40, or display it using chart paper or a transparency. Explain that this is a poem about the alphabet. Ask students to identify the letters *a, b, c, d, e,* and *f* in the selection, as well as a word that begins with each letter.

Ask Questions—Ask students if they know what their initials are. Tell them that initials are letters that stand for names.

Evoke Mood and Feeling—Ask students to look at the six letters featured in this selection, and choose their favorite letter. Ask them to explain why they like that letter. Is it the sound it makes? Is it the shape, such as a curvy or straight letter?

Letters

I like the letters of the alphabet.

A is for apple,
B is for blue.
C is for cow—
    moo, moo, moo.

D is for dragon,
E is for eat.
F is for finch—
    tweet, tweet, tweet.

Laura Portalupi

How did I read?

40   Fluency First!

Model Read and Read Together

Prosody—Read the selection aloud several times at a slow and steady speed. Point to the words as you read. Draw students' attention to the first letter in each alphabet word in the selection by pointing to it and stressing its sound. (i.e., "/a/ /a/ /a/ /pl/.")

Choral Reading—Move from modeling the poem to choral reading with students. Divide the class into two groups. Read the first line of the poem in unison. Then ask the first group to read lines 2–4. Have the second group read lines 6–8. Ask all students to join in to read the fifth and ninth lines of the poem together. Direct students to point to each word in the selection as they read it.

Practice—After modeling and reading the selection together, have students practice the selection alone, in pairs, or in small groups. Then encourage students to rehearse the selection by reading it aloud at home with family members.

Related Reading—If students are progressing well, introduce "*X, Y, Z.*" Have them begin by reciting the entire alphabet from A to W, then ending it with this rhyme.

A Related Selection
X, Y, Z

X, Y, and tumbledown Z,
The cat's in the cupboard
And can't see me.

Nursery rhyme

Coach and Rehearse

Paired Repeated Reading—Have students practice reading in small groups of four or five and individually for the group. While students are working, circulate and work with individual students, coaching them on reading with greater meaning and expression. Help students to place verbal emphasis on the initial letter sound of each alphabet word in the selection. ("B is for **b**lue.") After practice, ask a few students to perform the selection they practiced for the class.

Using the Audio CD—Students who are working together can go to the listening center to play the audio CD together and practice reading their parts. They can also record their reading of the selection and listen to it for self-evaluation.

Dress Rehearsal—Allow time for prepared students to present their readings before an audience of peers and teachers.

Word Work

Beginnings

1. Circle the picture whose name begins with the letter.

   d

   e

Write a Word

2. Write a word from the poem that begins with each letter.

   ª apple   ᵈ dragon

   ᵇ blue   ᵉ eat

   ᶜ cow   ᶠ finch

Build Skills and Strategies

Word and Letter Pair Concentration (see p. 98)—Select a set of six or eight alphabet letters to focus on for each round of this game. Help students make word bank cards for the set of letters by writing each letter on a card, and writing a word that begins with each letter on another card. Turn all the word and letter cards facedown; then each player turns over two cards at a time and says the words and/or letters that appear on the cards. Players try to make pairs by matching a letter card to the word that begins with that letter. If a pair is found, the player continues play until no more pairs are found.

Write Another Verse—As a class or in small groups, help students write additional verses for the selection. Remind students that in the selection, each letter of the alphabet is followed by a word that begins with that letter. Help them think of a sound to repeat three times for the fourth line of each verse. Create a draft for each verse, revise the draft, then make a final copy and post the entire selection (with the new verses you have written) in your classroom. An example follows:

> G is for goose,
> H is for hot.
> I is for ice cream:
> drip, drip, drip.

Independent Work—Assign the *Word Work* activities on page 41 of the Student Book. These activities will help students practice identifying the initial letter in words and picture names and can be completed at home or during another time.

Teacher's Notes—"Time to Rise"

Introduce and Discuss

"Time to Rise" provides an opportunity to analyze imagery and participate dramatically in a poem.

Introduce—Direct students to the selection on page 42, or display it using chart paper or a transparency. Tell students that they are going to read along as you read a poem to them. Ask them to listen for the two characters in the poem.

Ask Questions—Ask students if they like to sleep in late in the morning. Ask what makes them want to stay in bed or motivates them to get up early.

Evoke Mood and Feeling—Ask students to tell about a time they closely watched a bird or other animal. How did they feel looking at the animal? How close were they? Did the animal see them?

Model Read and Read Together

Prosody—Read the selection aloud several times. Point to the words as you read. Vary your speed, intonation, and expression, pausing at different spots. For example, pause dramatically after the third line. Use a "small voice" for the bird's voice.

Choral Reading—Move from modeling the poem to choral reading with students. Read the poem as a group. Ask students what kind of voice they think the birdie would have. Have them try to imitate the bird's voice.

Practice—After modeling and reading the selection together, have students practice the selection alone, in pairs, or in small groups. Encourage students to rehearse the selection at home with family members and friends.

Related Reading—If students are progressing well, introduce "Baby Nap." Ask students how it is different from the first selection. (It is about going to sleep, rather than waking up; it communicates a gentle, safe feeling, rather than a perky one.)

Time to Rise

A birdie with a yellow bill
Hopped upon the window sill,

Cocked his shining eye and said:
"Ain't you 'shamed you sleepy-head!"

Robert Louis Stevenson

How did I read?
☺ ☺ ☺

42   Fluency First!

A Related Selection
Baby Nap

This is baby ready for a nap.
Lay her down in her mother's lap.
Cover her up so she won't peep.
Rock her 'til she's fast asleep.

Anonymous

Coach and Rehearse

Paired Repeated Reading—Have students practice reading in small groups of four or five and individually for the group. While students are working, circulate and work with individual students, coaching them on reading with greater meaning and expression. Suggest they try to make the bird's voice light and bird-like. After practice, ask a few students to perform the selection they practiced for the class. They may perform alone or in small groups.

Using the Audio CD—Students who are working together can go to the listening center to play the audio CD together and practice reading their parts. They can also record their reading of the selection and listen to it for self-evaluation.

Dress Rehearsal—Allow time for prepared students to present their readings before an audience of peers and teachers.

Word Work

Words and Pictures

1. Circle the picture that matches the word.

birdie

window

Animals

2. Circle the picture that answers the question.

Who has a bill?

Who can hop?

Time to Rise **43**

Build Skills and Strategies

Word Ladder (see p. 100)—Guide students in creating new words derived from the word *head* in the poem.

WORD	CLUE
head	
read	Change the first letter to describe something you did with a book.
red	Drop a vowel to name a color.
bed	Change the first letter to describe something you sleep on.

Tableau (see p. 103)—Have pairs of students act out the poem. Ask one student to play the role of the sleepy-head. The other can play the role of the birdie on the windowsill. Have students discuss each interpretation of the poem.

Independent Work—Assign the *Word Work* activities on page 43 of the Student Book. These activities will help students connect word meaning to the written words and can be completed at home or during another time.

Perform and Celebrate

Designate a time on Day 5 for students to invite special guests and perform their favorite selection. Create a special setting for the performances. The reading selections need not be those that students have worked on during the week, but those they feel comfortable with and can perform with appropriate volume, expression, and meaning. Students may want to prepare special artwork or props for the selection they choose to perform.

Teacher's Notes—"Lost My Shoe"

Introduce and Discuss

"Lost My Shoe" provides students an opportunity to relate to the emotions created when something is lost and found.

Introduce—Direct students to the selection on page 44, or display it using chart paper or a transparency. Tell students that they are going to read along as you read a poem about something that could happen to anybody.

Ask Questions—Ask students to describe a time when they lost something. What was it? Did they find it? Where was it?

Evoke Mood and Feeling—How did students feel when they were looking for a lost item? Were they worried they wouldn't find it? How did they feel when they finally found the lost item?

Lost My Shoe

I lost my shoe.
Where can it be?

Under my bed?
Out by the tree?

Whew! I found it!
Silly old me.

Nancy Padak

How did I read?
☺ ☺ ☺

44 Fluency First!

Model Read and Read Together

Prosody—Read the selection aloud several times with different speeds, volume, intonation, and expression. Point to the words as you read them. Try lifting your voice at the end of the questions. You can also express relief with "Whew! I found it!" and chagrin with "Silly old me."

Choral Reading—Move from modeling the poem to choral reading with students. Read the poem as a group. Then divide up the poem in suitable ways so that different groups read different sections. For example, one group could read the lines that end with a period (statements). Another group can read the questions, and a third the exclamations. Encourage groups to use a voice appropriate for their type of sentence.

Practice—After modeling and reading the selection together, have students practice the selection alone, in pairs, or in small groups. Have them read the poem antiphonally, dividing the lines up among the groups of pairs differently. Encourage students to rehearse the selection at home with family and friends.

Related Reading—If students are progressing well, tell them you will read another poem about clothes called "A Great Outfit." Ask them what advice they would give the person in the poem.

A Related Selection
A Great Outfit

What should I wear today?
A bright pink cap
And long socks of gray,
I look in the mirror
and think, "No way!"

Laura Portalupi

Coach and Rehearse

Paired Repeated Reading—Have students practice reading in small groups of four or five and individually for the group. Circulate and work with individual students, coaching them on reading with greater meaning and expression. Challenge them to use different inflections at the end of each line, depending on the kind of sentence it is. After practice, ask a few students to perform the selection they practiced for the class. They may perform alone or in small groups.

Using the Audio CD—Students who are working together can go to the listening center to play the audio CD together and practice reading their parts. They can also record their reading of the selection and listen to it for self-evaluation.

Dress Rehearsal—Allow time for prepared students to present their readings before an audience of peers and teachers.

Word Work

Name the Picture

1. Draw a line to match each picture with a word. Trace the words.

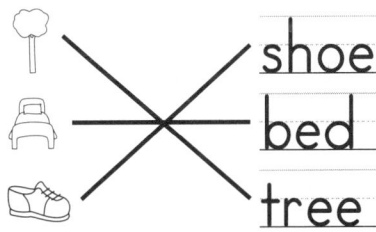

shoe
bed
tree

Where Is It?

2. Circle the picture that goes with the words.

under my bed

out by the tree

Lost My Shoe **45**

Build Skills and Strategies

Lost My…What?—Prepare cards with pictures and spellings of 10 objects kindergartners could lose, such as a sock, shirt, hat, pencil, book, etc. Have them read the first four lines of the poem, substituting the word on the card you show them for "shoe." For example,

> I lost my <u>hat</u>.
> Where can it be?
> Under my bed?
> Out by the tree?

Pair 'Em Up (see p. 94)—Present students with three words, two of which have the same beginning sound. Use at least one word from the poem with every group of three. Words to use include *shoe, bed, tree, found, silly,* and *me*. Sample triplets include:

- *shoe, tree, shout*
- *red, bed, bug*
- *sister, ant, silly*
- *trip, foot, tree*

Independent Work—Assign the *Word Work* activities on page 45 of the Student Book. These activities will give students the chance to read short words and phrases and can be completed at home or during another time.

Teacher's Notes—"A-Tisket, A-Tasket"

DAY 3

Introduce and Discuss

"A-Tisket, A-Tasket" provides students an opportunity to enjoy a common song and read a rhyming poem with repetitive phrases.

Introduce—Direct students to the selection on page 46, or display it using chart paper or a transparency. Ask students if they ever found something that belonged to someone else. How did the other person feel when the item was returned?

Ask Questions—Explain that *tisket* is an old-fashioned word for a flower bouquet. A *tasket* is a nonsense word used for rhyme. Discuss what comes to mind when they hear "green and yellow basket." What could they put in the basket?

Evoke Mood and Feeling—How might the person who wrote and dropped a letter feel? Ask students what they would do if they found the letter. Why?

A-Tisket, A-Tasket

A-tisket, a-tasket,
A green and yellow basket.

I wrote a letter to my love,
But on the way I dropped it.

I dropped it, I dropped it,
And on the way I dropped it.

A little boy picked it up,
And put it in his pocket.

Traditional song

How did I read?

46   Fluency First!

Model Read and Read Together

Prosody—Read the selection aloud several times at different speeds and with varying intonation and expression. Point to the words as you read. Adopt a singsongy intonation or one that adds drama to the story. Then sing the song. Have students critique the different ways you read the poem.

Choral Reading—Move from modeling the poem to choral reading with students. Read the poem as a group. Then read it using echo reading.

Practice—After modeling and reading the selection together, have students practice the selection alone, in pairs, or in small groups for a few minutes. Ask them to read the poem antiphonally, dividing the lines up in ways they choose themselves. Encourage students to rehearse the selection at home with family members and friends.

Related Reading—If students are progressing well, introduce "Humpty Dumpty." Ask them to retell the story in their own words.

A Related Selection
Humpty Dumpty

Humpty Dumpty sat on the wall,
Humpty Dumpty had a great fall.
All the king's horses
And all the king's men
Couldn't put Humpty Dumpty
Together again.

Mother Goose

Coach and Rehearse

Paired Repeated Reading—Have students practice reading in small groups of four or five and individually for the group. While students are working, circulate and work with individual students, coaching them on reading with greater meaning and expression. Ask them to repeat the poem with and without the melody. After practice, ask a few students to perform the selection they practiced for the class. They may perform alone or in small groups.

Using the Audio CD—Students who are working together can go to the listening center to play the audio CD together and practice reading their parts. They can also record their reading of the selection and listen to it for self-evaluation.

Dress Rehearsal—Allow time for prepared students to present their readings before an audience of peers and teachers.

Word Work

Beginnings

1. Draw a circle around the words that begin with the letter in the box.

l	wrote a (letter) to my (love)
d	I (dropped) it, I (dropped) it
p	(put) it in his (pocket)

Endings

2. Circle the picture that shows how the poem ends.

A-Tisket, A-Tasket **47**

Build Skills and Strategies

Odd Word Out (see p. 94)—Play this game using words from the poem. For example, when you say *yellow, yes,* and *white,* students should identify the odd word out, *white* (not a /y/ sound) or *yes* (not a color). Other words from the poem that would work in this game include:
- *little, letter, green*
- *basket, pocket, boy*
- *pocket, dropped, picked*

Have students explain why the word they pick is different from the other two.

Wordo (see pp. 100–101)—Provide students with a copy of the *Wordo* sheet and a set of markers. Have them randomly place the following words in each box: *green, yellow, basket, letter, love, dropped, little, boy,* and *pocket.* Then randomly call out the words, and have students place a marker over any word that was called and is on their sheet. If necessary, exaggerate beginning sounds or offer clues. Students win Wordo when they have three words covered in a row, a column, or a diagonal, or when they have covered the four corners.

Independent Work—Assign the *Word Work* activities on page 47 of the Student Book. These activities will help students hone their letter recognition and comprehension skills and can be completed at home or during another time.

Perform and Celebrate

Designate a time on Day 5 for students to invite special guests and perform their favorite selection. Create a special setting for the performances. The reading selections need not be those that students have worked on during the week, but those they feel comfortable with and can perform with appropriate volume, expression, and meaning. Students may want to prepare special artwork or props for the selection they choose to perform.

Teacher's Notes—"One, Two, Buckle My Shoe"

DAY 1

Introduce and Discuss

"One, Two, Buckle My Shoe" provides students an opportunity to count, to hear and use rhyming words, and to read using a beat or rhythm.

Introduce—Direct students to the selection on page 48, or display it using chart paper or a transparency. Tell the students they will read a nursery rhyme called "One, Two, Buckle My Shoe." Explain that to buckle a shoe means to fasten it.

Ask Questions—Ask students which two words rhyme in the title. Have them predict what other numbers might be included in the poem. Read the title again, pointing out that it is also the first line of the rhyme.

Evoke Mood and Feeling—Explain that part of the rhyme refers to a game played with sticks. Ask students what their favorite games are.

One, Two, Buckle My Shoe

One, two, buckle my shoe.
Three, four, shut the door.
Five, six, pick up sticks.
Seven, eight, lay them straight.
Nine, ten, do it again.

Nursery rhyme

How did I read? ☺ ☺ ☺

48 Fluency First!

Model Read and Read Together

Prosody—Read the selection aloud several times using a paced rhythm. Point to the words as you read. Gently tap your foot while you read to cue the students to the beat. As you read, emphasize the numbers that rhyme and their matching rhyming words.

Choral Reading—Move from modeling the poem to choral reading with students. Read the poem as a group. Then have students sit in a circle. Go around the circle having individuals read the number parts and the whole class read the phrases that follow.

Practice—After modeling and reading the poem together, have students practice the selection alone, in pairs, or in small groups for a few minutes. Encourage students to rehearse the selection at home with family members and friends.

Related Reading—If students are progressing well, ask them if the rhyme reminds them of any other rhyming poems that use numbers. Read "Four Potatoes in a Pot" using a beat, and emphasize the rhyming words. Ask the students to contrast the different ways that the two selections use numbers.

A Related Selection
Four Potatoes In a Pot

Four potatoes in a pot
Take one out and leave three hot.
Three potatoes in a pot,
Take one out and leave two hot.
Two potatoes in a pot,
Take one out and leave one hot.
One potato in a pot,
Take it out—
Nothing in the pot.

Nursery rhyme

Coach and Rehearse

Paired Repeated Reading—Have students practice reading in small groups of four or five and individually for the group. While students are working, circulate and work with individual students, coaching them on reading with greater meaning and expression. Encourage students to read with an evenly paced beat, emphasizing the rhyming words. After practice, ask a few students to perform the selection they practiced for the class. They may perform alone or in small groups.

Using the Audio CD—Students who are working together can go to the listening center to play the audio CD together and practice reading their parts. They can also record their reading of the selection and listen to it for self-evaluation.

Dress Rehearsal—Allow time for prepared students to present their readings before an audience of peers and teachers.

Word Work

Number Rhymes

1. Write a word from the box that rhymes with each picture.

four		two
two		six
six		four

First Things First

2. Circle the picture that shows what happened first.

One, Two, Buckle My Shoe **49**

Build Skills and Strategies

Copy Change (see p. 102)—Read the first line of the selection. Ask students to replace the phrase "buckle my shoe" with another rhyming phrase like "eat some stew" or "I love blue." Ask students to read the selection with the substitute text.

Word Pair Concentration (see p. 98)—Write out the number words *one* through *ten* on blank cards. Write their matching digits (1–10) on more cards. Mix up the cards and place them facedown. Have groups of students take turns flipping over two cards at a time. If the cards match, the student keeps them for one point. If the cards don't match, they are flipped back over again. Keep playing until all the cards are matched up and collected. The player with the most points wins.

Independent Work—Assign the *Word Work* activities on page 49 of the Student Book. These activities will reinforce rhyming words and comprehension skills and can be completed at home or during another time.

Teacher's Notes—"All Around the Mulberry Bush"

Introduce and Discuss

"All Around the Mulberry Bush" provides students an opportunity to adjust the volume of their voice and practice reading the word before an exclamation mark with an excited tone.

Introduce—Direct students to the selection on page 50, or display it using chart paper or a transparency. Tell students that they are going to read along as you sing and read the words to a song about a monkey and a weasel. Explain that a weasel is a small animal that looks like a rat and *'twas* means "it was".

Ask Questions—Ask students to raise their hands if they have ever seen monkey or a weasel. Ask them to imagine what a game of tag or chase would look like between these two animals.

Evoke Mood and Feeling—Find out from students if they have ever seen an animal being chased by another animal. Then how did they feel?

All Around the Mulberry Bush

All around the mulberry bush
The monkey chased the weasel.
The monkey thought 'twas all in fun.
Pop! goes the weasel.

A penny for a spool of thread,
A penny for a needle.
That's the way the money goes.
Pop! goes the weasel.

Traditional song

How did I read?

50　Fluency First!

Model Read and Read Together

Prosody—Read the selection aloud several times making your voice get louder with each line of the text. Point to the words as you read. Write the word *Pop!* on a large card. Hold up the card when you come to the word and shout out "Pop!"

Choral Reading—Move from modeling the poem to choral reading with students. Read the poem as a group chorally several times. Read it once echo style, then read and sing it together two or three times. Point to the words in the selection as you read it. Sing the song together.

Practice—After modeling and reading the selection together, have students practice the selection in pairs. Tell students to increase the volume of their voices with each line. Encourage students to rehearse the selection at home with family members and friends.

Related Reading—If students are progressing well, introduce "Here We Go 'Round the Mulberry Bush" and invite students to read along with you. Have students compare the activities that happen around a mulberry bush in the two songs.

A Related Selection
Here We Go 'Round the Mulberry Bush
(verses 1 & 2)

Here we go 'round the mulberry bush,
the mulberry bush,
the mulberry bush,
Here we go 'round the mulberry bush,
So early in the morning.

These are the chores we'll do this week,
do this week,
do this week,
These are the chores we'll do this week,
So early in the morning.

Traditional song

Coach and Rehearse

Paired Repeated Reading—Have students practice reading in small groups of four or five and individually for the group. Circulate and work with individual students, coaching them on reading with greater meaning and expression. Have them start out reading in a whisper and gradually increase the volume as they read each line. After practice, ask a few students to perform the selection they practiced for the class. They may perform alone or in small groups.

Using the Audio CD—Students who are working together can go to the listening center to play the audio CD together and practice reading their parts. They can also record their reading of the selection and listen to it for self-evaluation.

Dress Rehearsal—Allow time for prepared students to present their readings before an audience of peers and teachers.

Word Work

Shape Search

1. Write two words from the song that begin with the letter **m**.

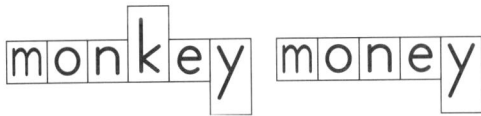

Match the Pictures

2. Draw a line to connect the things that go together in the poem.

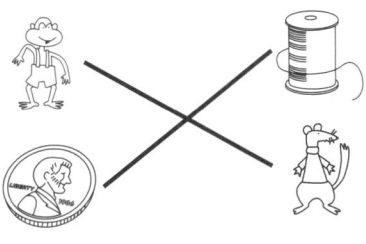

All Around the Mulberry Bush **51**

Build Skills and Strategies

Exclamation Points—Ask students to find the exclamation point in the last line of the poem. Explain that this mark indicates stress or emphasis. Copy the last line of the selection onto several strips of poster board and insert the following new words in the place of "Pop": Oh no!, Help!, Yikes! Have students read the new sentences stressing the word before the exclamation mark. Ask them to generate other words that could be used.

What's the Word? (see p. 95)—Play a "What's the Animal" version of the "What's the Word" game. Using a singsong voice and pausing between sounds, say the individual sounds or phonemes of the name of an animal, and ask students to blend them together. For example, say:
- This animal is a big cat.
- Here are the sounds: /t/, /ī/, /g/, /r/.
- What's the animal?

Independent Work—Assign the *Word Work* activities on page 51 of the Student Book. These activities will reinforce word recognition and comprehension skills and can be completed at home or during another time.

Perform and Celebrate

Designate a time on Day 5 for students to invite special guests and perform their favorite selection. Create a special setting for the performances. The reading selections need not be those that students have worked on during the week, but those they feel comfortable with and can perform with appropriate volume, expression, and meaning. Students may want to prepare special artwork or props for the selection they choose to perform.

Teacher's Notes—"Laundry Day"

DAY 1

Introduce and Discuss

"Laundry Day" provides students an opportunity to hear and read rhyming words as well as to see patterns in word families.

Introduce—Direct students to the selection on page 52, or display it using chart paper or a transparency. Tell the students that they are going to read along as you read the words to a rhyme about students who wash their dirty clothes. Explain that the word *laundry* describes clothing that needs to be cleaned.

Ask Questions—Ask students to describe how laundry is done at their home. Who usually does the laundry?

Evoke Mood and Feeling—Find out from students if they have ever gotten their clothes so dirty that they had to get changed and washed up right away?

Laundry Day

The children stand
    at the tub, tub, tub
The dirty clothes
    to rub, rub, rub.
When all is clean,
    and fit to be seen,
They'll dress in their finest
    and dance for the queen.

Traditional rhyme

How did I read?
☺ ☺ ☹

52 Fluency First!

Model Read and Read Together

Prosody—Read the selection aloud several times, speeding up or getting louder with the repeated words *tub* and *rub*. Point to the words as you read. Emphasize the rhyming words in the selection.

Choral Reading—Move from modeling the poem to choral reading with students. After reading the poem to your students, read it again as a group. Read it once echo style and then read it all together two or three times. Point to the words in the selection as you read it.

Practice—After modeling and reading the selection together, have students practice the selection in pairs. Encourage students to speed up at the repetitive words and to emphasize the rhyming words. Encourage students to rehearse the selection at home with family members and friends.

Related Reading—If students are progressing well, ask them if they noticed which words are written three times each. Have them point to the repeated words and read them with the students. Tell students you have another rhyme to share that repeats words three times. Introduce "We're Thirsty." Ask students what is the same about the words that are repeated. (They rhyme.)

A Related Selection
We're Thirsty!

The children stood at the sink, sink, sink
A glass of water to drink, drink, drink.
When their thirst was quenched and their drink was done
It was time to go out and have more fun.

Tim Rasinski

Coach and Rehearse

Paired Repeated Reading—Have students practice reading in small groups of four or five and individually for the group. While students are working, circulate and work with individual students, coaching them on reading with greater meaning and expression. Encourage students to increase the pace when they read the repetitive words. After practice, ask a few students to perform the selection they practiced for the class. They may perform alone or in small groups.

Using the Audio CD—Students who are working together can go to the listening center to play the audio CD together and practice reading their parts. They can also record their reading of the selection and listen to it for self-evaluation.

Dress Rehearsal—Allow time for prepared students to present their readings before an audience of peers and teachers.

Word Work

Again and Again

1. Write two words from the poem that rhyme.

tub   rub

What's Next?

2. What do the children do after they get dressed? Circle the picture.

Laundry Day **53**

Build Skills and Strategies

Word Families—Create a two-column work sheet with *–ub* at the top of the left column and *–een* at the top of the right column. Call out words: *rub, green, tub, seen, cub, teen.* Have students write the words in the appropriate column.

Closed Word Sort (see p. 98)—Make word cards for the words in the poem. Ask students to find:
- words that begin with the letter *d.*
- words that have the short *u* sound in them (say *"uuh"*).
- words that have the long *e* sound in them (say *"eeee"*).

Independent Work—Assign the *Word Work* activities on page 53 of the Student Book. These activities will reinforce rhyming, word recognition, and comprehension skills and can be completed at home or during another time.

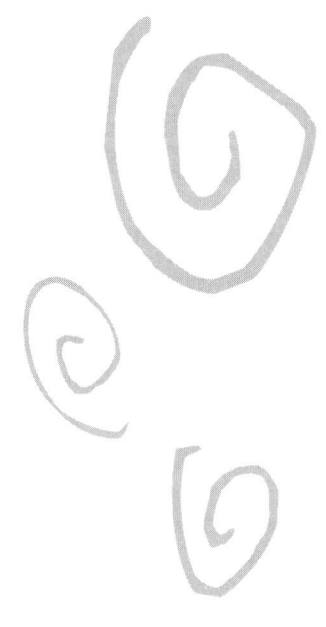

Teacher's Notes—"Teddy Bear, Teddy Bear"

Introduce and Discuss

"Teddy Bear, Teddy Bear" provides students an opportunity to repeat phrases and to hear and read rhyming words.

Introduce—Direct students to the selection on page 54, or display it using chart paper or a transparency. Tell the students that they are going to read along as you read the words to a jump rope rhyme. Explain that a jump rope rhyme is what students say out loud to keep a steady beat when jumping rope.

Ask Questions—Ask students if they have a teddy bear. Find out if the students have ever tried to teach their teddy bear to do things that they learned to do when they were younger.

Evoke Mood and Feeling—Ask students if their teddy bear is a special toy. If not, what toy is special? Who gave their special toy to them?

Teddy Bear, Teddy Bear

Teddy bear, Teddy bear,
    touch the ground.
Teddy bear, Teddy bear,
    turn around.

Teddy bear, Teddy bear,
    show your shoe.
Teddy bear, Teddy bear,
    that will do.

Teddy bear, Teddy bear,
    blow out the light.
Teddy bear, Teddy bear,
    say good night.

Jump rope rhyme

How did I read?
☺ ☺ ☹

54 Fluency First!

Model Read and Read Together

Prosody—Read the selection aloud several times while snapping your fingers. Keep the beat steady. Point to the words as you read. When you get to the part, "blow out the light," begin to soften your voice until the last line is just a whisper.

Choral Reading—Move from modeling the poem to choral reading with students. Read it once echo style and then read it all together two or three times. Snap your fingers as you read to keep the beat. Invite students to act out the parts as they read phrases like "turn around" and "show your shoe."

Practice—After modeling and reading the selection together, have students practice the selection in pairs. Encourage students to keep a steady beat and to gradually lower their voices until the last line is just a whisper. Direct students to rehearse the selection at home with family members and friends.

Related Reading—If students are progressing well, introduce "Teddy Bear." Ask students if both selections were intended to be read to the same teddy bear on a particular day, which would be read first and which would be read second? Why?

A Related Selection
Teddy Bear

Teddy Bear
sitting there
in my little rocking chair.
He waits all day
For me to say,
"Now it's time for us to play."

Karen McGuigan Brothers

Coach and Rehearse

Paired Repeated Reading—Have students practice reading in small groups of four or five and individually for the group. While students are working, circulate and work with individual students, coaching them on reading with greater meaning and expression. Encourage students to read the last few lines quietly. After practice, ask a few students to perform the selection they practiced for the class. They may perform alone or in small groups.

Using the Audio CD—Students who are working together can go to the listening center to play the audio CD together and practice reading their parts. They can also record their reading of the selection and listen to it for self-evaluation.

Dress Rehearsal—Allow time for prepared students to present their readings before an audience of peers and teachers.

Word Work

Spell the Name

1. Write words that tell who this poem is about.

   t e d d y   b e a r

Action Words

2. Draw a line to match the words with the pictures.

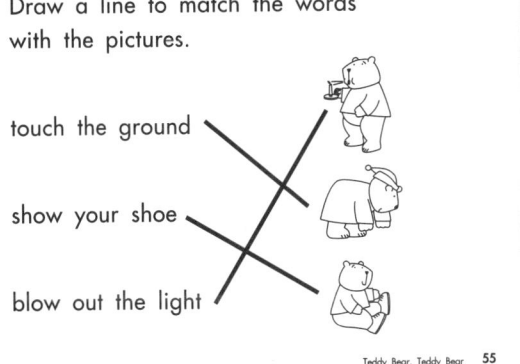

touch the ground

show your shoe

blow out the light

Teddy Bear, Teddy Bear **55**

Build Skills and Strategies

Rhyming Pairs—Read the selection again. Using one colored marker per rhyming pair, have students underline all the rhyming pairs of words from the text. Then copy the rhyming pairs onto blank cards, mix them up, and have students make pairs.

Odd Word Out (see p. 94)—Present students with three words, two of which rhyme. Ask students to identify the word that doesn't belong. For example, when you say *bear*, *chair*, and *day*, students should identify *day* as being the odd word out because it doesn't rhyme. Words from the poem that would work in this game include:
- *ground, around, shoe.*
- *light, night, book.*
- *shoe, around, do.*

Ask students to explain why the word they pick is different from the other two.

Independent Work—Assign the *Word Work* activities on page 55 of the Student Book. These activities will reinforce word recognition and comprehension skills and can be completed at home or during another time.

Perform and Celebrate

Designate a time on Day 5 for students to invite special guests and perform their favorite selection. Create a special setting for the performances. The reading selections need not be those that students have worked on during the week, but those they feel comfortable with and can perform with appropriate volume, expression, and meaning. Students may want to prepare special artwork or props for the selection they choose to perform.

Teacher's Notes—"I Love You"

Introduce and Discuss

"I Love You" familiarizes students with the relationships between objects and helps introduce rhyming words.

Introduce—Direct students to the selection on page 56, or display it using chart paper or a transparency. Explain that this selection is about love, and point to the word *love*. Ask students to identify the letters in the word *love*.

Ask Questions—Say the words *play* and *day*. Ask students what they notice about the words. (They rhyme.) Ask students to think of other words that rhyme with *play* and *day*. Then ask them to brainstorm other rhyming word pairs.

Evoke Mood and Feeling—Ask students to name something they love. Then ask them to name someone they love. Talk about how loving pizza is different from loving your dog.

I Love You

Cows love hay,
And night loves day.
Moms love May,
And I love you!

Dogs love pats,
And baseballs love bats.
Kittens love cats,
And I love you!

Tim Rasinski and Nancy Padak

How did I read?
☺ ☺ ☺

56   Fluency First!

Model Read and Read Together

Prosody—Read the selection aloud several times at a slow and steady speed. Point to the words as you read. Draw students' attention to the rhyming words in each verse by reading those words louder.

Choral Reading—Move from modeling the poem to choral reading with students. Have students sit in a circle. Go around the circle and invite each student to read one line of the poem individually. Then have students recite the fourth line of each verse chorally. Direct students to point to each word in the selection as they read it. Repeat the choral reading several times.

Practice—After modeling and reading the selection together, have students practice the selection alone, in pairs, or in small groups. Then encourage students to rehearse the selection by reading it aloud at home with family members.

Related Reading—If students are progressing well, introduce "My Bonnie Lies Over the Ocean," a song about lost love.

A Related Selection
My Bonnie Lies Over the Ocean

My Bonnie lies over the ocean,
My Bonnie lies over the sea.
My Bonnie lies over the ocean,
Please bring back my Bonnie to me.

Bring back,
Bring back,
Oh, bring back my Bonnie to me, to me.
Bring back,
Bring back,
Oh, bring back my Bonnie to me.

Traditional song

Coach and Rehearse

Paired Repeated Reading—Have students practice reading in small groups of four or five and individually for the group. Circulate and work with individual students, coaching them on reading with greater meaning and expression. Remind students to emphasize the rhyming words by raising their voices slightly as they read them. After practice, ask a few students to perform the selection they practiced for the class. They may perform alone or in small groups.

Using the Audio CD—Students who are working together can go to the listening center to play the audio CD together and practice reading their parts. They can also record their reading of the selection and listen to it for self-evaluation.

Dress Rehearsal—Allow time for prepared students to present their readings before an audience of peers and teachers.

Word Work

What Do They Love?

1. Draw lines to match each thing with something it loves.

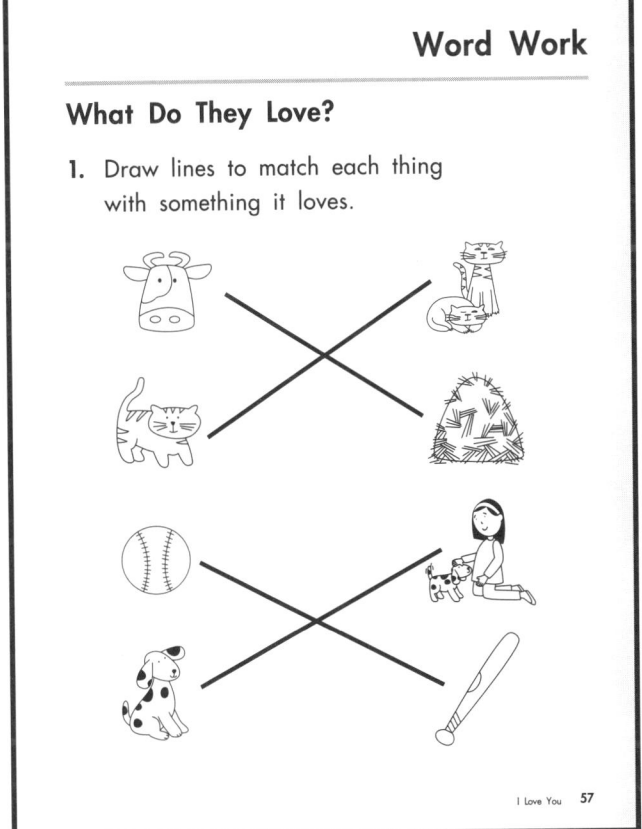

I Love You **57**

Build Skills and Strategies

Wordo (see pp. 100–101)—Provide students with a copy of the *Wordo* sheet and a set of markers. Have them randomly place the following words in each box: *love, hay, night, day, you, dogs, cats, bats,* and *kittens.* Then randomly call out the words and have students place a marker over any word that was called and is on their sheet. Students win Wordo when they have three words covered in a row, a column, or a diagonal, or when they have covered the four corners.

Word Ladder (see p. 100)—Guide students in creating new words derived from the word *cats* in the poem.

WORD	CLUE
cats	
rats	Change the first letter to describe small, city animals with long tails.
hats	Change the first letter to describe what people wear on their heads during winter.
hate	Change the last letter to get a word that means "strongly dislike."
late	Change the first letter to get a word that is the opposite of *early.*

Independent Work—Assign the *Word Work* activity on page 57 of the Student Book. This activity will help students pair up matching objects and can be completed at home or at another time.

Teacher's Notes—"Houses"

Introduce and Discuss

"Houses" offers a playful text to model expressive reading. Take time to talk about concepts and words that may be challenging for students, such as *bouquet of flowers*.

Introduce—Direct students to the selection on page 58, or display it on chart paper or a transparency. Tell students to follow along as you read a poem about different colored houses. Have them use their fingers to point to words as you read the text aloud.

Ask Questions—Ask students to share words that describe houses on their street. Record their responses on the board or on chart paper.

Evoke Mood and Feeling—Ask students to close their eyes and picture a bouquet of flowers. Have them describe the flowers in their bouquet. What colors are the flowers?

Houses

Just look down the street!
A blue house,
an orange house,
a yellow house,
a green house.
Like a bouquet of flowers.
The green one is ours!

Tony Johnston

How did I read?

58 Fluency First!

Model Read and Read Together

Prosody—Read the selection aloud several times. Point to the words as you read. Use a voice that shows amazement for the first and last lines. Exaggerate pauses after each line to give students the sense that you are walking down a street and looking at different houses.

Choral Reading—Move from modeling the poem to choral reading with students. After modeling it for your students, read it chorally several times. Recite it once echo style and then recite it all together two or three times.

Practice—After modeling and reading the selection together, have students work with a partner. Have one partner read the first line and the second read the next. Have students read the last line together. Encourage students to rehearse the selection at home with family members and friends.

Related Reading—Introduce "Casitas," the Spanish version of the poem. Have a guest speaker or a prepared student read the selection aloud. Remind students to listen to the rhythm of the poem. Have them listen carefully to how the first and last lines are read. Talk about how the readings are the same and different.

A Related Selection
Casitas

¡Asómate a la calle y mira!
Una casita azul
una casita anaranjada,
una casita amarilla,
una casita verde.
Como un ramillete.
¡La nuestra es la verde!

Tony Johnston

Coach and Rehearse

Build Skills and Strategies

Paired Repeated Reading—Have students practice reading in small groups of four or five and individually for the group. Circulate and work with individual students, coaching them on reading with greater meaning and expression. Encourage students to read the lines about the houses with more speed as they repeat the readings. After practice, ask a few students to perform the selection they practiced for the class. They may perform alone or in small groups.

Using the Audio CD—Students who are working together can go to the listening center to play the audio CD together and practice reading their parts. They can also record their reading of the selection and listen to it for self-evaluation.

Dress Rehearsal—Allow time for prepared students to present their readings before an audience of peers and teachers.

Phoneme Isolation—Ask students to listen to specific words found in the text, such as the word *house*. Have them identify the first sound heard in the word. Challenge them to think of other words that begin with the same sound, such as *him, her, home,* etc.

Describing Words—Discuss the color words in the poem. Explain that these words describe the houses. Talk about how the words provide more details about the houses. Allow time for students to use each of the color words in a sentence to describe something in the room. For example:
- I see a blue coat.
- I see an orange piece of chalk.
- I see a green crayon.

Independent Work—Assign the *Word Work* activities on page 59 of the Student Book. These activities will reinforce word recognition skills and can be completed at home or during another time.

Perform and Celebrate

Designate a time on Day 5 for students to invite special guests and perform their favorite selection. Create a special setting for the performances. The reading selections need not be those that students have worked on during the week, but those they feel comfortable with and can perform with appropriate volume, expression, and meaning. Students may want to prepare special artwork or props for the selection they choose to perform.

Word Work

Color the Words

1. Color the houses to match the words.

| blue | orange | yellow | green |

Match It

2. Draw a line to match each word with a picture. Trace the words.

house

street

flowers

Houses 59

Teacher's Notes—"I'm Kind of Scared"

DAY 1

Introduce and Discuss

"I'm Kind of Scared" provides students an opportunity to read rhythmical phrases and rhyming words.

Introduce—Direct students to the selection on page 60, or display it using chart paper or a transparency. Tell students to follow along as you read the poem aloud. Let them know the poem is about someone who is scared of the dark. Have students use their fingers to point to words as you read the text aloud.

Ask Questions—Ask students to talk about how they can change the sound of their voices to sound afraid or scared.

Evoke Mood and Feeling—Tell students to imagine they are in a dark room. Ask if they would be afraid or if they would they like the dark.

Model Read and Read Together

Prosody—Read the selection aloud several times. Point to the words as you read. Talk about how you grouped words together and paused between sentences. Model how you alter your voice to show the difference between a question and a statement and to show fear.

Choral Reading—Move from modeling the poem to choral reading with students. Read it chorally several times. Recite it once echo style and then recite it all together two or three times.

Practice—After modeling and reading the selection together, have students work with a partner. Demonstrate how to vary the speed of the reading. Have students read the text slowly and then a little faster. Ask them which speed makes sense for a poem. Encourage students to rehearse the selection at home with family members and friends.

Related Reading—If students are progressing well, tell them "Stop!" is about a different problem. Read the selection aloud. Have students suggest voices to support the new problem (a leaky faucet). Draw their attention to the rhythm and rhyme of the poem.

I'm Kind of Scared

Teddy Bear, Teddy Bear,
    are you still there?

Teddy Bear, Teddy Bear,
    I'm kind of scared.

It's awfully quiet and
    my room is dark.

Outside I hear a
    lonely dog bark.

Teddy Bear, Teddy Bear,
    are you still there?

Teddy Bear, Teddy Bear,
    I'm kind of scared.

Tim Rasinski

How did I read?

60   Fluency First!

A Related Selection
Stop!

Drip drop, drip drop.
Will the leak ever stop?
Call the police, call a cop.
Better yet, grab a mop!

Tim Rasinski

Coach and Rehearse

Build Skills and Strategies

Paired Repeated Reading—Have students practice reading in small groups of four or five and individually for the group. Circulate and work with individual students, coaching them on reading with greater meaning and expression. Remind students to change their voices to support the theme of being scared and to slow their voices down and read in a whisper. After practice, ask a few students to perform the selection they practiced for the class. They may perform alone or in small groups.

Using the Audio CD—Students who are working together can go to the listening center to play the audio CD together and practice reading their parts. They can also record their reading of the selection and listen to it for self-evaluation.

Dress Rehearsal—Allow time for prepared students to present their readings before an audience of peers and teachers.

Rhyming Words—Talk with students about rhyming words. Explain that rhyming words end with the same sounds. Have students reread the poem to find words that rhyme, such as *bear* and *there*, and *dark* and *bark*. Brainstorm other words that rhyme with *bear* and *bark*.

Question Marks—Tell students that some sentences tell something and some sentences ask questions. Ask volunteers to read the telling sentences. Have them point to the capital letter at the beginning of the sentence and the period at the end of the sentence. Ask volunteers to read the asking sentences. Have them point to the capital letter at the beginning of the sentence and the question mark at the end of the sentence.

Independent Work—Assign the *Word Work* activities on page 61 of the Student Book. These activities will reinforce word recognition and rhyming skills and can be completed at home or during another time.

Word Work

Match It

1. Draw a line to match the rhyming words.

dark   dog

log   bark

Draw It

2. Draw a picture of a toy that is special to you. Tell a friend why it is special.

Pictures will vary.

I'm Kind of Scared   **61**

Teacher's Notes—"Oh, How Lovely Is the Evening"

Introduce and Discuss

"Oh, How Lovely Is the Evening" provides an opportunity to read repetitive rhyming phrases with expression.

Introduce—Direct students to the selection on page 62, or display it using chart paper or a transparency. Bring in a bell. Have students ring and listen to the sounds of the bell. Let students know this poem has three parts. Take time to talk about words that may be unfamiliar to students, such as *lovely* and *sweetly*.

Ask Questions—Ask students to share sounds they hear during the evening. Encourage them to vary their voices to make interesting sounds for the animals or things they hear.

Evoke Mood and Feeling—Allow time for students to talk about things that happen in their homes that make an evening lovely or pleasant. Record students' responses.

Oh, How Lovely Is the Evening

Oh, how lovely is the evening,
Is the evening, is the evening,

When the bells are sweetly ringing,
Sweetly ringing,

Ding dong,
Ding dong,
Ding.

Traditional song

How did I read?
☺ ☺ ☹

62 Fluency First!

Model Read and Read Together

Prosody—Read the selection aloud several times. Point to the words as you read. Draw attention to how you change your voice to read each part. Share with students how you think about pleasant things as you read the words *lovely* and *sweetly*. Have them listen to the singsongy tone of your voice. Show how you think a bell might sound as you read the words *ding, dong*.

Choral Reading—Move from modeling the poem to choral reading with students. Read it chorally several times. Recite it once echo style and then recite it all together two or three times.

Practice—Have students form small groups to practice reading the selection. Provide support as necessary. Encourage students to rehearse the selection at home with family members and friends.

Related Reading—If students are progressing well, introduce "Oh, How Noisy Is the Evening." This poem is about street noises. Briefly discuss ways to change the tone and speed of your voice to support the new theme. Allow time for students to identify parts that are the same and different between the two selections.

A Related Selection
Oh, How Noisy Is the Evening

Cars and trucks are always beeping, always beeping	Beep, beep Beep, beep. Beep.
Wake me sometimes when I'm sleeping, when I'm sleeping	*Karen McGuigan Brothers*

Coach and Rehearse

Paired Repeated Reading—Have students practice reading in small groups of four or five and individually for the group. Circulate and work with individual students, coaching them on reading with greater meaning and expression. Encourage students to use a soft, controlled voice to reflect the quiet loveliness of the evening. After practice, ask a few students to perform the selection alone or in small groups.

Using the Audio CD—Students who are working together can go to the listening center to play the audio CD together and practice reading their parts. They can also record their reading of the selection and listen to it for self-evaluation.

Dress Rehearsal—Allow time for prepared students to present their readings before an audience of peers and teachers. Post a sign-up sheet for students who want to participate.

Word Work

Draw It

1. Draw a picture to match the words.

bell	bells
Picture should include one bell.	Picture should include more than one bell.

Shape Search

2. Write the word from the poem that tells how the bells ring.

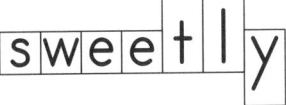

Oh, How Lovely Is the Evening **63**

Build Skills and Strategies

Syllables—Select words from the poem, such as *bells, lovely, evening,* and *dong.* Write the words on index cards. Give each student three counters. Read a word aloud. Ask students to use the counters to show how many syllables or beats they hear in each word. Allow time for students to share their thinking.

Plurals—Ask students to identify a word that shows more than one. Draw attention to how the letter *s* is added to the word *bell* to make it plural. Write a list of words on the board, such as *star, bird,* and *car.* Ask volunteers to add the letter *s* to make the word show more than one. Invite them to draw pictures to show the meaning of each word.

Independent Work—Assign the *Word Work* activities on page 63 of the Student Book. These activities will reinforce word recognition and comprehension skills and can be completed at home or during another time.

Perform and Celebrate

Designate a time on Day 5 for students to invite special guests and perform their favorite selection. Create a special setting for the performances. The reading selections need not be those that students have worked on during the week, but those they feel comfortable with and can perform with appropriate volume, expression, and meaning. Students may want to prepare special artwork or props for the selection they choose to perform.

Teacher's Notes—"I'm Glad"

Introduce and Discuss

"I'm Glad" offers a context in which to model reading a text in phrases instead of word-by-word.

Introduce—Direct students to the selection on page 64, or display it using chart paper or a transparency. Use a bologna sandwich to discuss the concept of being "sandwiched in between." Talk about how the objects are squished together like a sandwich.

Ask Questions—Ask students what things they see when they are outside. What do they see when they look up? Down? What do they see that makes them happy?

Evoke Mood and Feeling—Allow time for students to talk about things they feel good about when they are outside in the fresh air. Encourage them to share stories about things they like to do.

I'm Glad

I'm glad the sky
    is painted blue
And earth is painted green
With such a lot
    of nice fresh air
All sandwiched in between.

Mother Goose

How did I read?

64   Fluency First!

Model Read and Read Together

Prosody—Read the selection aloud several times. Point to the words as you read. Have students listen as you read the text word-by-word and then in phrases. Talk about the differences between the two readings. Have students identify which reading sounds better and why.

Choral Reading—Move from modeling the poem to choral reading with students. Recite it once echo style and then recite it all together two or three times.

Practice—After modeling and reading the selection together, ask students to read the poem together as a choral reading. Have volunteers suggest sound effects that support the reading, such as a tambourine jingle for the sky and a drum rap for the earth. Encourage students to take the poem home to share with family members and friends.

Related Reading—If students are progressing well, introduce "I Caught a Fish" to model another expressive reading. Alter the speed and volume of your voice as you read the series of numbers. Maintain a quick-paced rhythm as you read the poem aloud. Encourage students to read the selection along with you.

A Related Selection
I Caught a Fish

One, two, three, four, five,
I caught a fish alive.
Why did you let it go?
Because it bit my finger so.

Mother Goose

Coach and Rehearse

Paired Repeated Reading—Have students practice reading in small groups of four or five and individually for the group. Circulate and work with individual students, coaching them on reading with greater meaning and expression. Remind students about the rhythm of the poem. Have them change the volume of their voices and the speed of the reading to determine what reading works best. After practice, ask a few students to perform the selection they practiced for the class.

Using the Audio CD—Students who are working together can go to the listening center to play the audio CD together and practice reading their parts. They can also record their reading of the selection and listen to it for self-evaluation.

Dress Rehearsal—Allow time for prepared students to present their readings before an audience of peers and teachers.

Word Work

Picture the Words

1. Draw something you see in the sky. Write a title for your drawing.

Pictures will vary.

I'm Glad **65**

Build Skills and Strategies

Initial Blends—Draw students' attention to the word *glad*. Ask a volunteer to identify the two letters that make the /gl/ sound. Say the word aloud together. List other words students know that begin with the /gl/ sound, such as *glove, glue, glitter,* and *glow*. Have students use the words in sentences and then put them on the Word Wall.

Color Words—Make a two-column chart. Write the words *blue* and *green* with a matching crayon or marker, one word in each column. Challenge students to find objects in the classroom that are these colors. Ask them to draw and label the objects in the correct column.

Independent Work—Assign the *Word Work* activity on page 65 of the Student Book. This activity will reinforce comprehension skills and can be completed at home or during another time.

Teacher's Notes—"Love Somebody"

DAY 3

Introduce and Discuss

"Love Somebody" gives students the chance to read a rhythmic text.

Introduce—Direct students to the selection on page 66, or display it using chart paper or a transparency. Talk about how people express affection in different ways, such as giving a hug or helping out around the house.

Ask Questions—Ask students what words and feelings they think of when they think about love. Draw a large heart shape on the board and write student's words in the shape. Talk about words that might be unfamiliar to students, such as *somebody* and *hope*.

Evoke Mood and Feeling—Allow time for students to share how they show somebody they love them. Ask them how they feel when somebody cares and loves them.

Love Somebody

Love somebody, yes I do,
Love somebody, yes I do,
Love somebody, yes I do,

And I hope somebody loves me too.

Love somebody, can't guess who,
Love somebody, can't guess who,
Love somebody, can't guess who,

And I hope somebody loves me too.

Traditional song

How did I read?

66   Fluency First!

Model Read and Read Together

Prosody—Read the selection aloud several times. Point to the words as you read. Vary the speed and tone of your voice. Read it fast and loud the first time. Then read it again slowly and quietly. Talk about how the changes in your voice change the meaning of the reading.

Choral Reading—Move from modeling the poem to choral reading with students. Read it chorally several times. Recite it once echo style and then recite it all together two or three times.

Practice—After modeling and reading the selection together, have students read specific lines in the song. Assign a line to each student. Have them read their lines aloud. Direct students to read the lines differently each time. Encourage students to practice reading the text at home to family members and friends.

Related Reading—If students are progressing well, share "Curly Locks, Curly Locks" with students. Tell them this poem is addressed to the author's love. Have students listen carefully to the rhythm of the text as you read it aloud. Work with students to compare and contrast the ideas found in the two selections.

A Related Selection
Curly Locks, Curly Locks

Curly Locks, Curly Locks,
Will you be mine?
You shall not wash dishes,
Nor feed the swine,
But sit on a cushion
And sew a fine seam,
And sup upon strawberries,
Sugar, and cream.

Nursery rhyme

Coach and Rehearse

Paired Repeated Reading—Have students practice reading in small groups of four or five and individually for the group. While students are working, circulate and work with individual students, coaching them on reading with greater meaning and expression. Have them read softly and then increase the volume for each additional reading. After practice, ask a few students to perform the selection they practiced for the class. They may perform alone or in small groups.

Using the Audio CD—Students who are working together can go to the listening center to play the audio CD together and practice reading their parts. They can also record their reading of the selection and listen to it for self-evaluation.

Dress Rehearsal—Allow time for prepared students to present their readings before an audience of peers and teachers.

Word Work

Shape Search

1. Write a word from the song that begins the same as **lock**.

Draw a Picture

2. Draw a picture of someone you love.

Pictures will vary.

Love Somebody **67**

Build Skills and Strategies

Phoneme Segmentation—Draw students' attention to sounds in words. Say words from the text aloud. Have students tell how many sounds they hear, such as two sounds in the word *too*, three sounds in the word *yes*, and two sounds in the word *me*.

Compound Words—Write the word *somebody* on the board. Tell students that somebody is made up of two smaller words, *some* and *body*. Explain that this is called a compound word. Have a volunteer underline the two words in *somebody*. Generate a list of other compound words students know. Provide hints if necessary, such as, "This word is a walk on the side of a road" (sidewalk). Draw their attention to the two words that are put together to make the compound word.

Independent Work—Assign the *Word Work* activities on page 67 of the Student Book. These activities will reinforce word recognition and comprehension skills and can be completed at home or during another time.

Perform and Celebrate

Designate a time on Day 5 for students to invite special guests and perform their favorite selection. Create a special setting for the performances. The reading selections need not be those that students have worked on during the week, but those they feel comfortable with and can perform with appropriate volume, expression, and meaning. Students may want to prepare special artwork or props for the selection they choose to perform.

Teachers Notes—"Baa, Baa, Black Sheep"

DAY 1

Introduce and Discuss

"Baa, Baa, Black Sheep" provides students an opportunity to use their voices to distinguish between two voices in a nursery rhyme.

Introduce—Direct students to the selection on page 68, or display it using chart paper or a transparency. Explain that the master and dame in the nursery rhyme are the man and woman who own the sheep.

Ask Questions—Ask students what the curly hair on a sheep is called. Make sure students understand that the fleece and fabric are both called wool.

Evoke Mood and Feeling—Discuss what students know about sheep. Ask what sort of animals are sheep? How do they act? What sounds do they make? Make a topic web to record students' responses or let several volunteers pretend to be sheep for a minute or so.

Baa, Baa, Black Sheep

Baa, baa, black sheep,
Have you any wool?
Yes, sir, yes, sir,
Three bags full.

One for my master,
One for my dame,
And one for the little boy
Who lives in the lane.

Baa, baa, black sheep,
Have you any wool?
Yes, sir, yes, sir,
Three bags full.

Nursery rhyme

How did I read?

68   Fluency First!

Model Read and Read Together

Prosody—Read the selection aloud at least twice, varying your tone, pace, and volume to differentiate between the words the questioner uses and the sheep's responses. Make the phrase "baa, baa" sound as much like a sheep as you can. Point to the words as you read. Then sing the song.

Choral Reading—Move from modeling the nursery rhyme to choral reading with students. Read the rhyme line by line and have students echo read after you. Direct students to point to each word as they read it. Then sing the rhyme as a class or have a group of volunteers sing it.

Practice—After modeling and reading the selection together, have students practice the selection alone, in pairs, or in small groups. Direct students to use their voices to differentiate between the questioner and the sheep. Then tell the students to rehearse the selection at home with family members and friends.

Related Reading—If students are progressing well, introduce "Little Bo-Peep." Have students discuss similarities of the selections, such as both being rhymes about sheep.

A Related Selection
Little Bo-Peep

Little Bo Peep has lost her sheep,
And can't tell where to find them,
Leave them alone, and they'll come home
Wagging their tails behind them.

Mother Goose

Coach and Rehearse

Paired Repeated Reading—Have students practice reading in small groups of four or five and individually for the group. While students are working, circulate and work with individual students, coaching them on reading with greater meaning and expression. If necessary, help students distinguish between the questioner's and the sheep's lines. After practice, ask a few students to perform the selection they practiced for the class. They may perform alone or in small groups.

Using the Audio CD—Students who are working together can go to the listening center to play the audio CD together and practice reading their parts. They can also record their reading of the selection and listen to it for self-evaluation.

Dress Rehearsal—Allow time for prepared students to present their readings before an audience of peers and teachers.

Build Skills and Strategies

Match the Letter—Have students find the words in the nursery rhyme that begin with the letter *b*. Ask students to write the title "Words with *B/b*" at the top of a sheet of paper. Then have them look through "Baa, Baa, Black Sheep" and write all the words that start with *b* (*Baa, bags, black, boy*). Tell them to write each word with *b* only once even if it is repeated several times.

Syllable Clap—Invite students to clap for each syllable they hear as you read "Baa, Baa, Black Sheep" slowly and rhythmically. Challenge students to identify the two words that have more than one syllable (*master, little*).

Independent Work—Assign the *Word Work* activities on page 69 of the student book. These activities will reinforce word recognition and comprehension skills and can be completed at home or during another time.

Word Work

Shape Search

1. Write four words from the poem that begin with **b**.

| b | a | a |

| b | l | a | c | k |

| b | o | y |

| b | a | g | s |

How Many?

2. How many bags of wool are full? Circle the number.

one   two   (three)   four

Baa, Baa, Black Sheep **69**

Teacher's Notes—Knock, Knock Jokes

DAY 3

Introduce and Discuss

Knock, Knock Jokes help students read conversationally or individually using two voices. Students can also use their voices to indicate different types of end punctuation.

Introduce—Direct students to the selection on page 70, or display it using chart paper or a transparency. Tell students that they are going to read along and listen as you read knock, knock jokes. Explain that a knock knock joke always contains the same back-and-forth wording between a joke teller and a listener.

Ask Questions—Point to the first line and tell students that the first line of a knock, knock joke is "knock knock." Ask them to predict what the second line could be.

Evoke Mood and Feeling—Ask students how jokes make them feel. Do they like to tell jokes?

Knock, Knock Jokes

Knock, knock.
    Who's there?
Cowsgo
    Cowsgo who?
No, they don't. Cows go "moo!"

Knock, knock.
    Who's there?
A bee
    A bee who?
A-B-C-D-E-F-G

Author unknown

How did I read?
☺ ☺ ☹

70   Fluency First!

Model Read and Read Together

Prosody—Read the jokes aloud several times. Point to the words as you read. Tell the jokes using two different voices to say the alternative lines.

Choral Reading—Move from modeling the poem to choral reading with students. Divide the class into two groups: the people telling the jokes and their audience. Have the joke tellers read the first, third, and fifth lines chorally, and the audience members read the second and forth lines chorally.

Practice—After modeling and reading the selection together, pair up students and have them pick one of the selections to practice. One student is the joke teller while the other student is the audience, and they should read the lines accordingly. Encourage students to rehearse the selection at home with family members and friends.

Related Reading—If students are progressing well, read the related selection aloud. Ask students to identify the lines that the joke teller says and the lines that the audience says. Find the words that are the same in both selections.

A Related Selection
Knock, Knock Jokes

Knock, knock.
    Who's there?
Boo
    Boo who?
You don't have to cry about it!

Knock, knock.
    Who's there?
Spell
    Spell who?
W—H—O

Author unknown

Coach and Rehearse

Paired Repeated Reading—Have students practice reading in small groups of four or five and individually for the group. Circulate and work with individual students, coaching them on reading with greater meaning and expression. Demonstrate how a reader can use his or her voice to match this punctuation and add expression to the jokes. After practice, ask a few students to perform the selection they practiced for the class. They may perform alone or in small groups.

Using the Audio CD—Students who are working together can go to the listening center to play the audio CD together and practice reading their parts. They can also record their reading of the selection and listen to it for self-evaluation.

Dress Rehearsal—Allow time for prepared students to present their readings before an audience of peers and teachers.

Word Work

Match It

1. Draw a line to match each picture with a word. Trace the word.

knock

buzz

moo

ABC Order

2. Write the letters in order.

B   E   A   G   F   D   C

A B C D E F G

Knock, Knock Jokes 71

Build Skills and Strategies

I Say (see p. 95)—Use this game to play with words. Say one simple word from the text, and students say another word that rhymes:
- I say *knock*. You say ___.
- I say *who*. You say ___.

Making and Writing Words (see pp. 96–97)—Help students make up their own increasingly complex words by manipulating a limited set of letters. Reproduce the *Making and Writing Words* sheet and distribute to students.

Special Word: about
Vowels: a, o, u   **Consonants:** b, t

Clues
to—rhymes with *shoe,* is only two letters
but—rhymes with *cut*
bat—something you use to hit a ball
tub—a place to take a bath
tuba—a large musical instrument

Special Word
about—He was ____ ready to start work.

Independent Work—Assign the *Word Work* activities on page 71 of the Student Book. These activities will help students recognize words and practice alphabetization and can be completed at home or during another time.

Perform and Celebrate

Designate a time on Day 5 for students to invite special guests and perform their favorite selection. Create a special setting for the performances. The reading selections need not be those that students have worked on during the week, but those they feel comfortable with and can perform with appropriate volume, expression, and meaning. Students may want to prepare special artwork or props for the selection they choose to perform.

Teacher's Notes—"Chores"

DAY 1

Introduce and Discuss

"Chores" helps students listen for and practice reading rhyming words.

Introduce—Direct students to the selection on page 72, or display it using chart paper or a transparency. Tell students that they are going to read along and listen as you read a rhyming poem called "Chores."

Ask Questions—Point to and tell students that the title of this poem is "Chores." Ask them to think of a word that rhymes with chores. Chart a few of these words.

Evoke Mood and Feeling—Ask students to describe their most favorite and least favorite household chores. Record a few of the best and worst chores on the board.

Model Read and Read Together

Prosody—Read the selection aloud several times. Point to the words as you read. Use simple motions to add meaning to the words. For example, as you read the first line, hold up one finger to indicate "one little chore."

Choral Reading—Move from modeling the poem to choral reading with students. Divide the class into four groups. Ask the first group to read the first line, the second group to read the second line, and so on. Then read the entire selection together as a class. Point to the words as you read them, and emphasize the rhyming words with your voice.

Practice—After modeling and reading the selection together, have students practice the selection alone, in pairs, or in small groups. Help students use simple motions to bring more meaning to their selection. Encourage students to rehearse the selection at home with family members and friends.

Related Reading—If students are progressing well, introduce "Middle Man" aloud. Ask students to compare the rhyming words in the two selections. Point out that the rhyming words in "Middle Man" all contain the *–ort* word family, and the rhyming words in "Chores" contain two different word families that sound the same: *–our* and *–ore.*

A Related Selection
Middle Man

There once was a man from Davenport
Not too tall and not too short.
Mostly of the medium sort
That in-the-middle man from Davenport.

Tim Rasinski

Chores

My mother gave me
    one little chore—
To buy some eggs
    at the grocery store.

I bought the eggs
    and a little more—
Chocolate cookies
    and milk to pour.

Tim Rasinski

How did I read?

72 Fluency First!

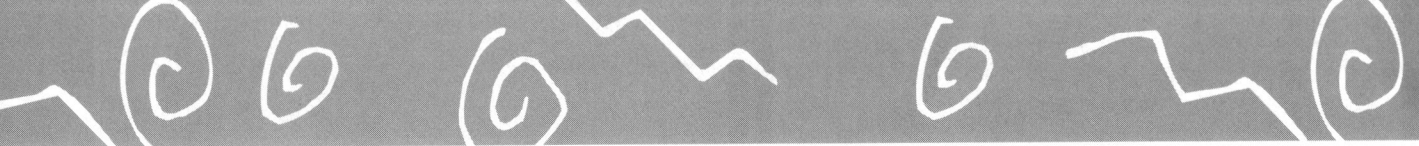

Coach and Rehearse

Paired Repeated Reading—Have students practice reading in small groups of four or five and individually for the group. While students are working, circulate and work with individual students, coaching them on reading with greater meaning and expression. Encourage students to read each line as a coherent phrase instead of word-for-word. After practice, ask a few students to perform the selection alone or in small groups.

Using the Audio CD—Students who are working together can go to the listening center to play the audio CD together and practice reading their parts. They can also record their reading of the selection and listen to it for self-evaluation.

Dress Rehearsal—Allow time for prepared students to present their readings before an audience of peers and teachers. Post a sign-up sheet for students who want to participate.

Word Work

Rhyming Words

1. Circle three words from the poem that rhyme with **chore**.

 store more milk pour

Sounds Like?

2. Circle the pictures whose names start with **m**.

 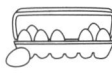

Chores **73**

Build Skills and Strategies

Odd Word Out (see p. 94)—Present students with three words, two of which rhyme. Ask students to identify the word that doesn't belong. For example, when you say *chore, toad,* and *store,* students should identify *toad* as being the odd word out. Discuss the word families in the rhyming words.

- *gave, save, dive*
- *bought, eight, fought*
- *made, mate, late*

Play "Word Pair Concentration" (see p. 98)—Help students make word bank cards for the rhyming words from the selection. Brainstorm additional words that rhyme with these words, and make cards for them. Then make doubles of all the rhyming word bank cards. Turn all the word cards facedown, and then invite a player to turn over two cards at a time and say the words on the cards. Players who find a matching pair of rhyming words keep the pair and continue to turn cards over until no more pairs are found.

Independent Work—Assign the *Word Work* activities on page 73 of the Student Book. These activities will help students identify rhyming words and recognize the initial consonant sounds and can be completed at home or during another time.

Teacher's Notes—"Yam Is Yummy"

Introduce and Discuss

"Yam Is Yummy" helps students read with rhythm and experiment with reading the same poem at different speeds.

Introduce—Direct students to the selection on page 74, or display it using chart paper or a transparency. Tell students that this poem talks about yams, which are sweet potatoes that can be prepared and enjoyed in many different ways.

Ask Questions—Point to the word *yam*, and survey students to see how many of them have ever eaten a yam. Ask those who have tried yams to describe what they taste like. Write students' descriptive words on the board.

Evoke Mood and Feeling—Ask students to describe a time that they tried a food for the first time. Did they like the new food? Record some of the foods on the board or chart paper.

Yam Is Yummy

Yam is yummy,
Yam is yummy,
Yam is yum-yummy
When it's in my tummy.

Uzo Unobagha

How did I read?

Model Read and Read Together

Prosody—Read the selection aloud several times at a slow and steady speed. Point to the words as you read. Beat a drum, clap your hands, or snap your fingers to the rhythm as you read to help students feel the beat of the poem. Then read the selection at a faster pace and beat out the rhythm accordingly. Finally, read at an exaggeratedly slow pace.

Choral Reading—Move from modeling the poem to choral reading with students. As a group, echo read the selection at a slow speed, medium speed, and fast speed. Encourage one student (or half the class) to keep rhythm on a drum or by tapping a desk or table as the remaining students read. Point to the words in the selection as you read.

Practice—After modeling and reading the selection together, pair up students and have them practice the selection alone, in pairs, or small groups for a few minutes. Encourage students to rehearse the selection at home with family members and friends.

Related Reading—If students are progressing well, introduce "Grandma Makes Me Plantain Flakes" aloud. Explain that a plantain is a fruit like a banana. Ask students to identify the rhyming words in this selection, and compare the placement of the rhyming words to the rhyming words in the first selection.

A Related Selection
Grandma Makes Me Plantain Flakes

Grandma makes me plantain flakes,
Grandma bakes me plantain cakes,
Plantain flakes and plantain cakes,
All day Grandma makes and bakes.

Uzo Unobagha

Coach and Rehearse

Paired Repeated Reading—Have students practice reading in small groups of four or five and individually for the group. While students are working, circulate and work with individual students, coaching them on reading with greater meaning and expression. Have students emphasize the initial sound that *y* makes in *yam* and *yummy*. After practice, ask a few students to perform the selection alone or in small groups.

Using the Audio CD—Students who are working together can go to the listening center to play the audio CD together and practice reading their parts. They can also record their reading of the selection and listen to it for self-evaluation.

Dress Rehearsal—Allow time for prepared students to present their readings before an audience of peers and teachers. Post a sign-up sheet for students who want to participate.

Word Work

Endings

1. Circle one picture whose name ends with the same sound as **yam**.

  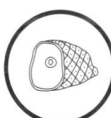

Count the Syllables

2. Count the number of syllables you hear in each word. Write the number on the line.

yam   my _____

yummy 2   tummy 2

Build Skills and Strategies

Presto-Chango (see p. 95)—Sound substitution requires students to subtract, add, or substitute sounds from existing words. Ask questions such as:
- What word will you get if you change the *t* in *tummy* to *m*?
- Add *p* to *in*. What word will you get?

List-Group-Label (see p. 99)—Ask students to brainstorm words related to *eating*, such as *tasty, lunch, apples, dishes,* etc. Record the words on the board. Then examine the words and identify groups of words that are related in some way. Label the words according to their commonality.

Independent Work—Assign the *Word Work* activities on page 75 of the Student Book. These activities will help students listen for final consonant sounds and count syllables in words and can be completed at home or during another time.

Perform and Celebrate

Designate a time on Day 5 for students to invite special guests and perform their favorite selection. Create a special setting for the performances. The reading selections need not be those that students have worked on during the week, but those they feel comfortable with and can perform with appropriate volume, expression, and meaning. Students may want to prepare special artwork or props for the selection they choose to perform.

Teacher's Notes—"Three Little Bees"

DAY 1

Introduce and Discuss

"Three Little Bees" provides students an opportunity to emphasize rhyming words as they count to three in a counting rhyme.

Introduce—Direct students to the selection on page 76, or display it using chart paper or a transparency. Read the title and have students count to three.

Ask Questions—Ask students what bees look like and what sound they make. Draw a bee on the board or let a volunteer do so. Then ask, Why do bees stop at flowers? What food do bees make from what they find there?

Evoke Mood and Feeling—Have volunteers tell you some information they know about bees: where they live, why they are important, reasons people should be cautious of them, and so on.

Model Read and Read Together

Prosody—Read the selection aloud several times, varying your pace and volume. Point to the words as you read. Hold up one, two, and three fingers of your other hand as you read the words *one, two,* and *three*. Open your hand and wave your fingers as the bees fly away at the end of the rhyme.

Choral Reading—Move from modeling the counting rhyme to choral reading with students. Read the rhyme line by line and have students echo read after you. Have students point to each word as they read it. Have them hold up fingers of their other hand at the appropriate points in the rhyme as you did when you read it to them.

Practice—Have students practice the selection alone, in pairs, or in small groups for a few minutes. Encourage students to count with their fingers. Then tell the students to rehearse the selection at home with family members and friends.

Related Reading—If students are progressing well, introduce "One Little Flower, One Little Bee." Guide students in finding similarities and differences between poems.

Three Little Bees

One little bee blew and flew,
He met a friend,
   and that made two.

Two little bees, busy as could be,
Along came another,
   and that made three.

Three little bees working every hour,
Buzz away, bees,
   and find another flower.

Counting rhyme

How did I read?

76   Fluency First!

A Related Selection
One Little Flower, One Little Bee

One little flower, one little bee.
One little blue bird, high in the tree.
One little brown bear smiling at me.
One is the number I like, you see.

Mother Goose

Coach and Rehearse

Paired Repeated Reading—Have students practice reading in small groups of four or five and individually for the group. While students are working, circulate and work with individual students, coaching them on reading with greater meaning and expression. After practice, ask a few students to perform the selection they practiced for the class. They may perform alone or in small groups.

Using the Audio CD—Students who are working together can go to the listening center to play the audio CD together and practice reading their parts. They can also record their reading of the selection and listen to it for self-evaluation.

Dress Rehearsal—Allow time for prepared students to present their readings before an audience of peers and teachers. Post a sign-up sheet for students who want to participate.

Word Work

Shape Search

1. Write three words from the poem that begin with **b**.

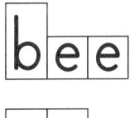 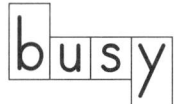

What Happens Last?

2. What happens last? Circle the correct picture.

Three Little Bees **77**

Build Skills and Strategies

Rhyming Words—Have students identify the rhyming word pairs in "One Little Bee" (*flew, two; be, three; hour, flower*). Give them hints such as the following to help them think of another word that rhymes with each pair.

- This rhyming word is the sound a cow makes (*moo*).
- This rhyming word is a word I use for myself (*me*).
- This rhyming word is a part of a castle (*tower*).

Independent Work—Assign the *Word Work* activity on page 77 of the student book. This activity will reinforce word recognition and comprehension skills and can be completed at home or during another time.

Teacher's Notes—"School Is Out"

Introduce and Discuss

"School Is Out" helps students read in pairs and use different voices to express different moods.

Introduce—Direct students to the selection on page 78, or display it using chart paper or a transparency. Tell students that they are going to read along and listen as you read a rhyming poem. Read and point to the title of the poem, and ask students what they think the poem will be about.

Ask Questions—Ask students what their favorite summertime activities are. Chart their responses. Then add your summer pastimes to the list.

Evoke Mood and Feeling—Ask students how they feel about school being out. What are they excited about? What will they miss? Record some of their statements on the board.

School Is Out

Watch T.V.
Read a book.
Catch a fish
on a hook.

Take a walk
or take a run.
School is out—
it's time for fun!

Karen McGuigan Brothers

How did I read?
☺ ☺ ☹

78   Fluency First!

Model Read and Read Together

Prosody—Read the selection aloud several times, alternating between two different voices, line by line, as if two people are reading it. Point to the words as you read. Read as if the two readers are arguing back and forth. Then read as if the two readers are in agreement about the summer activities. Finally, read as if one reader is excited and happy, and the other one is sad and disappointed.

Choral Reading—Move from modeling the poem to choral reading with students. Split the class into two groups to read chorally. Assign each group a voice or tone, and ask them to use that voice as they read. Point to the words in the selection as they are read.

Practice—After modeling and reading the selection together, have students pair up and practice reading one or both of the selections. Ask each pair of students to choose two different voices to use as they read. Encourage students to rehearse the selection at home with family members and friends.

Related Reading—If students are progressing well, introduce "Summertime" by reading it aloud. Ask students how the second selection is the same as or different from the first selection. Read the selection using different voices (e.g., upbeat, sad, expressionless, angry), and ask students which voice seems to match the words in the selection best.

A Related Selection
Summertime

Summer summer almost here.
Summertime is really near.
Of this fact I'm surely clear.
Summertime's the best time of year.

Tim Rasinski

Coach and Rehearse

Paired Repeated Reading—Have students practice reading in small groups of four or five and individually for the group. Circulate and work with individual students, coaching them on reading with greater meaning and expression. Assign each group of students two voices (such as enthusiastic, disappointed, angry, etc.) to use as they practice reading. After practice, ask a few students to perform the selection they practiced for the class. They may perform alone or in small groups.

Using the Audio CD—Students who are working together can go to the listening center to play the audio CD together and practice reading their parts. They can also record their reading of the selection and listen to it for self-evaluation.

Dress Rehearsal—Allow time for prepared students to present their readings before an audience of peers and teachers.

Word Work

Shape Search

1. Write two words from the poem that end with **ook**.

b	o	o	k

h	o	o	k

Rhyme Time

2. Circle the picture whose name rhymes with the word.

    cook

    wish

    run

Build Skills and Strategies

Pair 'Em Up (see p. 94)—Present students with three words, two of which have the same ending sound, like *look, fish,* and *hook.* Ask students which two words have the same ending sound. Then ask them to isolate and say the sound. Other words to use include:
- *run, walk, fun.*
- *book, hook, run.*
- *fun, fish, wish.*

Agree? Disagree? Why? (see p. 102)—Ask students to write or dictate a journal entry agreeing or disagreeing with the selection. Encourage them to finish the following prompt: "I agree (or disagree) with the poem 'School Is Out' because…" Students could also use this journal entry to describe or list things they enjoy doing during their summer vacation.

Independent Work—Assign the *Word Work* activities on page 79 of the Student Book. These activities will help students identify word shapes and words that rhyme and can be completed at home or during another time.

Perform and Celebrate

Designate a time on Day 5 for students to invite special guests and perform their favorite selection. Create a special setting for the performances. The reading selections need not be those that students have worked on during the week, but those they feel comfortable with and can perform with appropriate volume, expression, and meaning. Students may want to prepare special artwork or props for the selection they choose to perform.

Appendix

This appendix provides a description of skill-building games and activities that will develop student's phonemic and phonological awareness, decoding, vocabulary, and comprehension skills. It also contains reproducible black-line masters for implementing the informal assessment components of the program.

Activities to Promote Phonemic and Phonological Awareness

Pair 'Em Up

Present students with three words, two of which have the same beginning sound like *bat, cat, cane*. Ask students which two words have the same beginning sound. Then ask them to explain. You can also play this game with middle and ending sounds or rhyming words.

Odd Word Out

This game is like "Pair 'Em Up" except that students identify the word that doesn't belong. For example, when you say *bat, cat*, and *cane*, students might identify either *bat* or *cane* as the odd word. Be sure to ask children for their reasons.

Change the Word

Say a simple word from the text. Direct students to change the beginning sound to make a new word. For example, you could say, "My word is *coat*. Change the /k/ to /b/. What is your word?" Repeat with several other words from the text.

I Say

Use this game to play with words. You say one simple word from the text, and students say another word that rhymes: "I say *cat*. You say ___." "I say *bee*. You say ___." Repeat with several other words.

Presto-Chango

Sound substitution requires students to subtract, add, or substitute sounds from existing words. Ask questions such as, "What word do you get when you take the /k/ off of *cat*? when you add /m/ to *at*."

What's the Word?

Using a singsong voice and pausing between sounds, say individual sounds from a word and ask students to blend the sounds together to form a word. For example, you might say, "I'm thinking of something we do at night. Here are the sounds: /s/, /l/, /ē/, and /p/. What's the word?"

Split the Word

Once children can do "What's the Word?" easily, try this activity. Say a word and ask students to break it up into individual sounds. For example, you might say *cat* and the children should respond with /k/, /a/, and /t/.

Activities to Promote Vocabulary Development

Making and Writing Words

Students make up their own increasingly complex words by manipulating a limited set of letters. To prepare for the activity, duplicate enough *Making and Writing Words (MWW)* sheets (see at right) for each student. Then select a special word of between five and eight letters from the text. Determine a set of additional words that can be made from the letters of this special word, and develop clues for the words. Anagram Web sites such as *www.wordsmith.org/anagram* are good sources for words. Have students write the vowels and consonants in the appropriate boxes at the top of the MWW sheet. Then provide them with clues to the words they will write in each box on the sheet. The final box is always reserved for the special word. Then ask students to think and write other words that follow the same letter patterns (e.g., in the same word family using any letter). Here is an example.

Special Word
catfish

Vowels   Consonants
a, i   c, f, h, s, t

Use the clues below to help students create the word. Be sure to provide other clues, such as antonyms, synonyms, number of letters, or other word features as needed.

fish—an animal that lives in water and has gills
cat—an animal that meows
sit—something you do on a chair
fast—moving quickly
mast—a large pole that holds a sail on a sailboat

Special Word
catfish—a fish that looks like it has whiskers

Some Possible Bonus Words
dish, wish, swish, squish
sat, rat, bat, fat, hat, mat, pat
bit, fit, hit, kit, pit
past, last, vast, mast
ash, clash, mash, flash, bash, dash

Making and Writing Words

Name _____   Date _____

Write the assigned letters in the correct box.

Vowels	Consonants

Write a word in each box based on the clues you are given.

1.	4.
2.	5.
3.	6. Special Word

Create bonus words using similar letter patterns.

7.	9.
8.	10.

Activities to Promote Vocabulary Development *continued*

Word Banks

Word banks are collections of words that students collect on their own from the passage. The words are written on small cards or slips of paper. Children can keep their words in envelopes, index card boxes, or other small containers. Using word bank words, you and the children can play the following games:

Word War

In this variation of the card game *War*, each player has a deck of word cards. (One child can deal the word bank deck out evenly to all players.) In turn, each player uncovers the card at the top of his or her deck, says the word, and lays it on the table. The player who plays the word with the most letters and says the word correctly wins the round and takes the other players' cards. In cases of a tie, each player involved in the tie uncovers a second card and says it. In this tie-breaking round, the player with the most letters wins all the cards played in the entire round. Another tie results in another tie-breaking round, and so forth.

Word Pair Concentration

This involves making doubles of Word Bank cards. Turn all the words facedown; then each player turns over two cards at a time and says the words as they are turned. Players try to find pairs of words. If a pair is found, the player continues play until no more pairs are found.

Open Word Sort

Invite children to group their words in ways that make sense to them. Then direct partners to examine the groups to try to figure out how each group was sorted.

Closed Word Sort

Each student selects a dozen words and sorts their words into piles: consonant blends vs. no consonant blends; long vowel sounds, short vowel sounds, both, and neither; nouns, verbs, and neither; words that are things and words that are not things; and words with one syllable, two syllables, and more than two syllables. The possibilities are endless. Select sorting options that are related to skills or strategies you are teaching elsewhere in your literacy curriculum.

List-Group-Label

Identify the central concept or general topic of the text.

- Students work with partners to brainstorm as many related words as possible in two minutes. For example, if the topic is flowers, words might include, *smell, stem, petal, rose,* etc.
- Partners examine the collected words, identify groups of words that are related in some way, and provide labels for these groups of words such as "types of flowers," "parts of flowers," etc.

Conclude the activity with whole-group sharing. You might also ask students to create webs or semantic maps of their words.

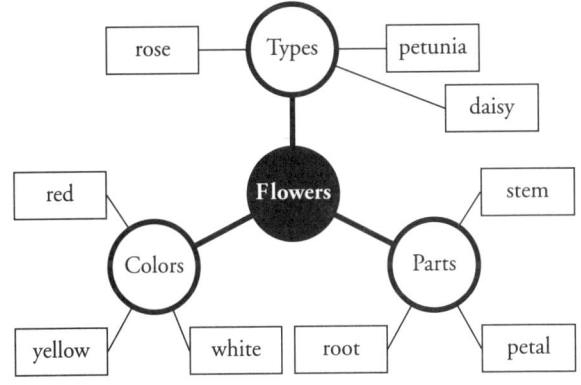

An alternative is to make this a whole-group activity, in which case you will record children's contributions on the board or chart paper.

Word Wall

Post interesting words that you and your students choose from each selection on a wall or bulletin board in your classroom. Practice reading the words regularly with students. Discuss the various meanings of the words and encourage students to use the words in their own speech and writing.

About Vocabulary Learning

What kinds of practice develop good reading?
The *Report of the National Reading Panel* says:

Reading comprehension is a cognitive process that integrates complex skills and cannot be understood without examining the critical role of vocabulary learning and instruction and its development. Active interactive strategic processes are critically necessary to the development of reading comprehension.

Activities to Promote Vocabulary Development *continued*

Word Ladder

This activity begins with you directing the students to create a numbered list and write the first word of the ladder next to 1. Then guide students in making a new word for each number. In word ladders, the first and next word are related somehow. The word ladder below demonstrates the process. Consider demonstrating the process using large magnetic letters to form the first two words.

WORD	CLUE
pig	
big	Change the first letter to describe something that is not small.
wig	Change the first letter to name hair that you wear as a costume.
dig	Change the first letter to name what you do to make a hole in the ground.
jig	Change the first letter to name a dance.

Wordo

This game is a variation of Bingo. Blank grids (see page at right) are randomly filled with words by the students that they have been practicing. Using no particular order, you or a game leader calls out a word's definition or some unique element of the word (e.g., "this is a one-syllable word that has a silent *e*"), or a sentence leaving the target word out. (e.g., "The mother bear fed the ___.") Players find and cover up their word squares as students identify and call out the word. Dried lima beans are excellent inexpensive markers for covering words. The first player with a covered line of words running across, down, or diagonally, or all four corners covered is the winner.

rain	bug	bike
cat	sun	rock
cub	foot	boat

About Fluency and Word-Recognition Skills

What kinds of practice develop fluency?
The *Report of the National Reading Panel* says:

Fluent readers can read text with speed, accuracy, and proper expression. Fluency depends on well-developed word recognition skills . . . . It is generally acknowledged that fluency is a critical component of skilled reading.

Wordo

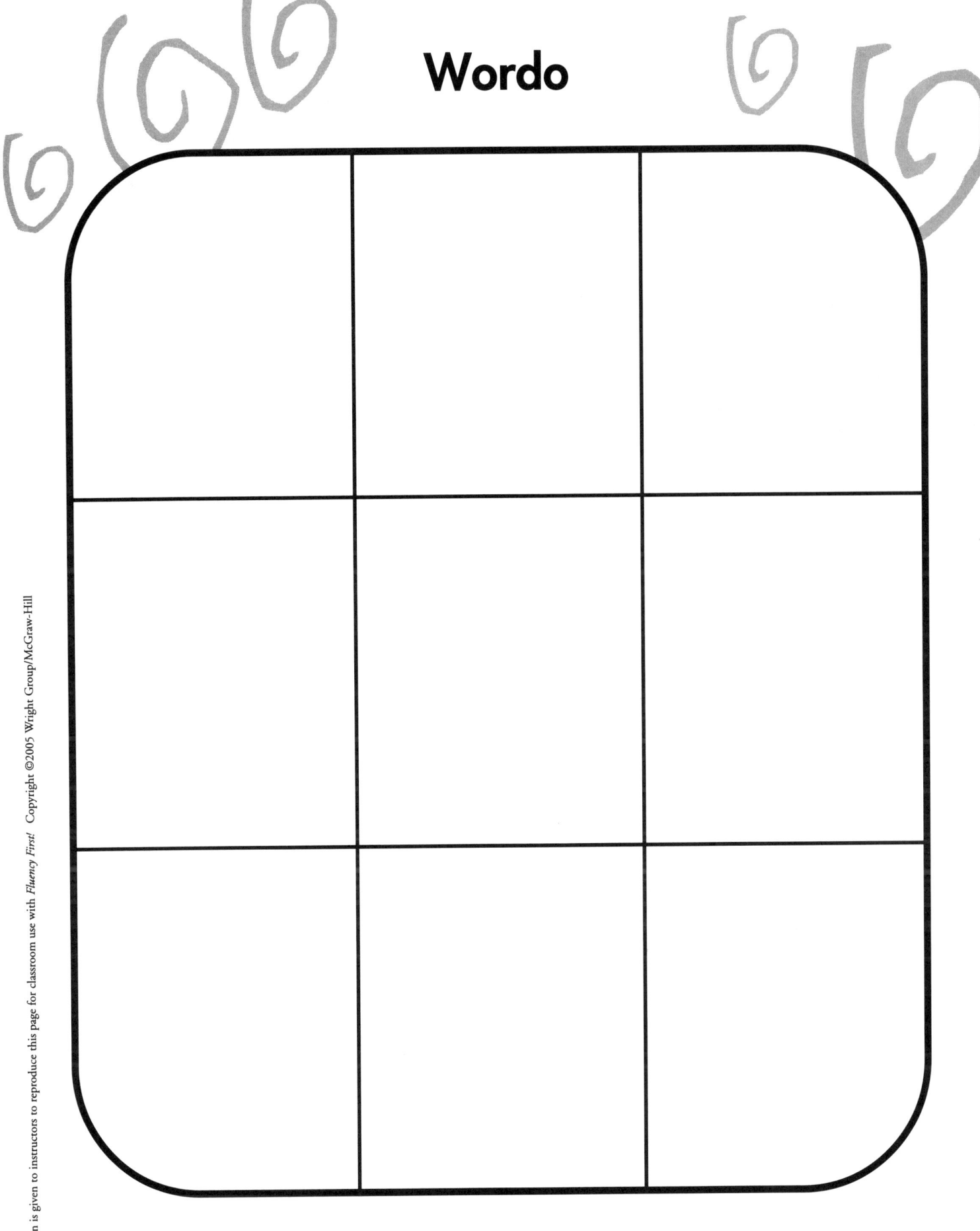

Activities to Promote Comprehension

Prevoke

Before reading, select several (10–12) words from the text; these should be words children recognize with little difficulty. Then select two or three categories for the words, such as *people*, *places*, and *things* or *characters*, *setting*, and *plot*. Before reading the text, children work with partners to categorize the words. A brief class discussion focuses on how children categorized the words or what they expect the text to be about. After reading the text, partners return to their original categorization and make changes.

Agree? Disagree? Why?

Create a sentence or two that is related to the ideas in the text and expresses ideas children could agree or disagree with. Direct children to consider the sentences, decide on their own opinions, and formulate reasons for their decisions. These can be shared orally, in children's journals, or both.

Young children enjoy moving to different spots in the room according to whether they agree or disagree. When groups assemble, they will discuss reasons for their opinions and select a few to share with the other group.

Copy Change

Children work with partners, in small groups, or as a whole group to create another version of the text using the author's framework. For example, Bill Martin's *Brown Bear, Brown Bear* could become "[principal's name, principal's name], what do you see? I see a student looking at me." or "Teddy bear, teddy bear, what do you see? I see a happy child looking at me."

These comprehension activities will get students thinking deeply about the meaning of the selection through prediction, imagery, discussion, vocabulary, and writing.

Sketch to Stretch

Give children a minute or two to sketch something related to the text. Then direct them to form groups of three, share their sketches with each other, and talk about how the sketch is related to the text.

Tableau

Have groups of students draw pictures of the selection using their bodies in freeze frames. These freeze frames are called *tableaux*. Give groups a few minutes to think of ways they can create a scene or theme represented in the selection they have just read. Then have one group after another perform their tableaux by turning themselves into silent statues. The rest of the class tries to determine the scene or meaning that is being portrayed. The planning involved and figuring out the tableaux are great for helping students learn to interpret a text.

About Comprehension Skills

What kinds of practice develop comprehension? The *Report of the National Reading Panel* says:

Comprehension strategies are specific procedures that guide students to become aware of how well they are comprehending.... Instruction in comprehension strategies is carried out by a classroom teacher who demonstrates, models, or guides the reader in their acquisition or use.

Journal Activities

These quick writing activities enhance children's comprehension.

- Tell *who* and *what happened.*

- Tell about how something or someone in the text is the same or different from something or someone else.

- Write three sentences: one for the beginning, middle, and end of the story.

- Order a list of important ideas.

- Write two sentences: one for the problem and one for the solution, as described in the text.

Activities to Promote Comprehension
continued

Important Words

After they have read a text, ask partners to identify the two or three most important words from the text. Then invite a whole-class discussion on the words that students have selected and their reasons for doing so. If you use journals, asking individuals to select and justify their own most important word is a good activity for follow-up.

About Comprehension Skills

What kinds of practice develop comprehension? The *Report of the National Reading* Panel says:

Comprehension instruction can effectively motivate and teach readers to learn and to use comprehension strategies that benefit the reader.

Graphic Organizers

Graphic Organizers can help students visually organize and summarize information from a text. Partners might work to complete the graphics together, or you can guide the whole group by drawing it on the board or a piece of chart paper.

Compare and Contrast: Have students consider similarities and differences between two things (e.g., two characters in a text, a character in the text and themselves, two texts, and so on) by using a Venn diagram.

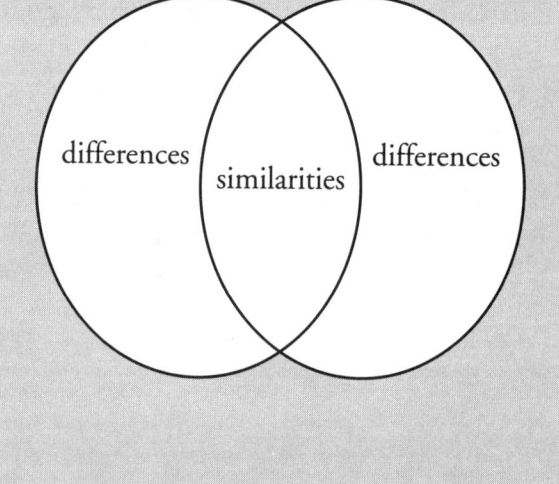

Identify Main Idea and Details: Using a herringbone, students find answers to "who?" "what?" "when?" "where?" "why?" and "how?" as related to a text. They write these answers on the "bones" of the Herringbone chart. Then they combine these into a sentence that expresses the main idea.

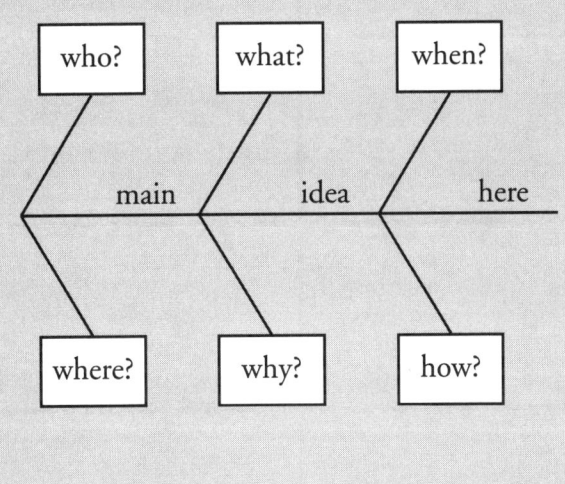

Sequence: A simple sequence chart helps students organize story events. Initially, lead students in a discussion of events and complete the chart together.

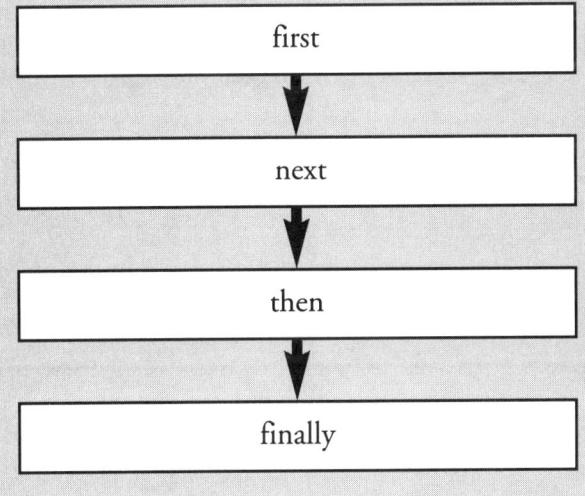

Identify Story Elements: Students can make notes about characters, setting, problem, solution, important events, etc. using a story map.

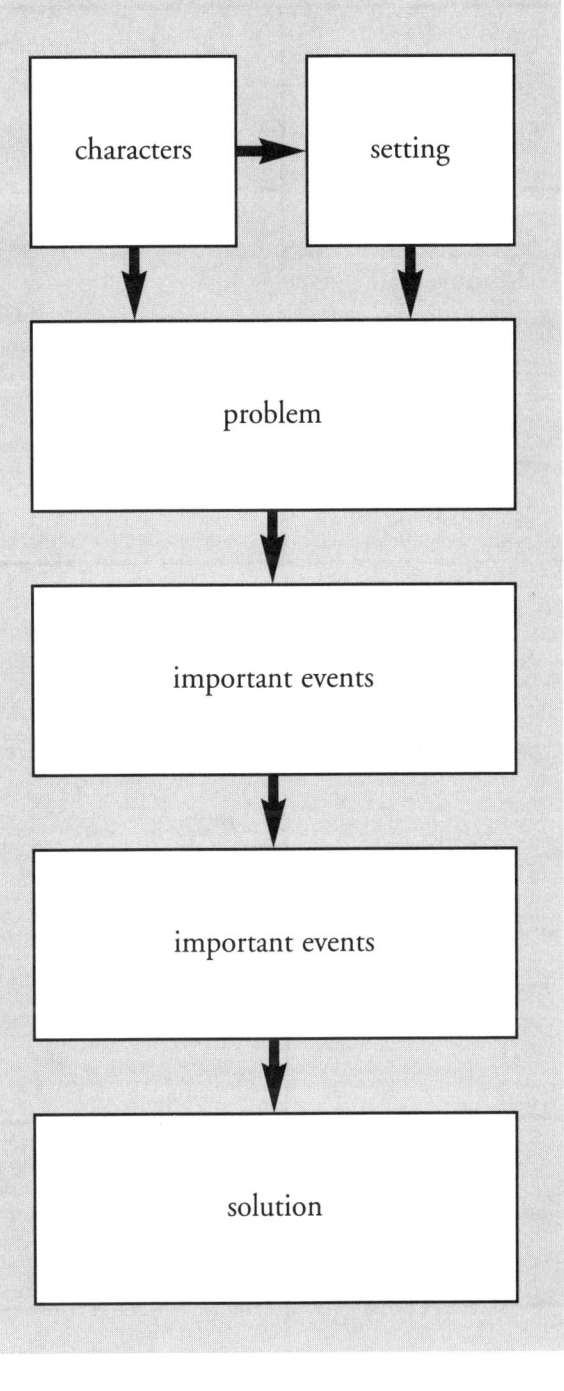

Fluency Observation Chart

Selection _____   Date _____

	Student's Name	Student's Name	Student's Name
Reading Rate			
Accuracy			
Expression			
Volume			
Clarity			
Eye Contact/Gestures			
Overall Fluency			

Fluency Continua

Student's Name _____   Date _____

Selection _____

Place an X on the continuum at each assessment; record the date above.

Reading Rate	Outstanding	Satisfactory	Unsatisfactory

Accuracy	Outstanding	Satisfactory	Unsatisfactory

Expression	Outstanding	Satisfactory	Unsatisfactory

Volume	Outstanding	Satisfactory	Unsatisfactory

Clarity	Outstanding	Satisfactory	Unsatisfactory

Eye Contact/Gestures	Outstanding	Satisfactory	Unsatisfactory

Overall Fluency	Outstanding	Satisfactory	Unsatisfactory

Fluency Checklist

Student's Name

Date

Selection

	Outstanding	Satisfactory	Unsatisfactory
Reading Rate			
Accuracy			
Expression			
Volume			
Clarity			
Eye Contact/Gestures			
Overall Fluency			

Self-Assessment

Name _____ Date _____

Selection _____ Level _____

My reading was fluent.	☺	☺	😐
I read most of the words right.	☺	☺	😐
I read with good expression.	☺	☺	😐
My reading sounded smooth and easy.	☺	☺	😐
I spoke loud enough for people to hear me.	☺	☺	😐
My voice was clear.	☺	☺	😐
My listener could understand what I read.	☺	☺	😐

Bibliography

Allington, R. L. 1983. Fluency: The neglected reading goal. *The Reading Teacher 36*: 556–561.

Chard, D.J., Vaughn, S., & Tyler, B. 2002. A synthesis of research on effective interventions for building fluency with elementary students with learning disabilities. *Journal of Learning Disabilitie, 35*: 386–406.

Donahue, P.L., Finnegan, R.J., Lutkus, A.D., Allen, N.L., & Cambell, J.R. 2001. *The nation's Report card for reading: Fourth grade.* Washington, DC: National Center for Educational Statistics.

Dowhower, S. L. 1987. Effects of repeated reading on second-grade transitional readers' fluency and comprehension. *Reading Research Quarterly 22*: 389–407.

Hasbrouck, J. E., & Tindal, G. 1992. Curriculum-based oral reading fluency norms for students in Grades 2 through 5. *Teaching Exceptional Children 24*: 41–44.

Heckelman, R. G. 1969. A neurological impress method of reading instruction. *Academic Therapy 4*: 277–282.

Hoffman, J. V. 1987. Rethinking the role of oral reading in basal instruction. *Elementary School Journal 87*: 367–373.

Hoffman, J. V., O'Neal, S., Kastler, L., Clements, R., Segel, K., & Nash, M.F. 1984. Guided oral reading and miscue focused verbal feedback in second-grade classrooms. *Reading Research Quarterly 19*: 367–384.

Knapp, N. F., & Winsor, A. P. 1998. A reading apprenticeship for delayed primary readers. *Reading Research and Instruction 38*: 13–29.

Koskinen, P. S., Blum, I. H., Bisson, S. A., Phillips, S. M., Creamer, T. S., & Baker, T. K. 1999. Shared reading, books, and audiotapes: Supporting diverse students in school and at home. *The Reading Teacher 52*: 430–444.

Koskinen, P. S., Blum, I. H., Bisson, S. A., Phillips, S. M., Creamer, T. S., & Baker, T. K. 2000. Book access, shared reading, and audio models: The effects of supporting the literacy learning of linguistically diverse students in home and school. *Journal of Educational Psychology 92*: 23–36.

Kuhn, M.R., & Stahl, S. A. 2000. *Fluency: A review of developmental and remedial practices* (CIERA Rep. No. 2-008). Ann Arbor, MI: Center for the Improvement of Early Reading Achievement.

Mercer, C. C., Campbell, K. U., Miller, M. D., Mercer, K. D., & Lane, H. B. 2000. Effects of a reading fluency intervention for middle schoolers with specific learning disabilities. *Learning Disabilities: Research and Practice 15(4)*: 179–189.

Millin, S. K., & Rinehart, S. D. 1999. Some of the benefits of readers theater participation for second-grade Title I readers. *Reading Research and Instruction 39*: 71–88.

Morris, D., & Nelson, L. 1992. Supported oral reading with low achieving second graders. *Reading Research and Instruction 32*: 49–63.

National Reading Panel. 2000. *Report of the National Reading Panel: Teaching children to read. Report of the subgroups.* Washington, DC: U.S. Department of Health and Human Services, National Institutes of Health.

Opitz, M. F., & Rasinski, T. V. 1998. *Good-bye Round Robin: 25 effective oral reading strategies.* Portsmouth, NH: Heinemann.

Pinnell, G. S., Pikulski, J. J., Wixson, K. K., Campbell, J. R., Gough, P. B., & Beatty, A. S. 1995. *Listening to children read aloud.* Washington, DC: U. S. Department of Education, Office of Educational Research and Improvement.

Rasinski, T. V. 1989. Fluency for everyone: Incorporating fluency in the classroom. *The Reading Teacher 42*: 690–693.

Rasinski, T.V. 1990. Effects of repeated reading and listening-while-reading on reading fluency. *Journal of Educational Research 83*: 147–150.

Rasinski, T. V. 2003. *The fluent reader: Oral reading strategies for building word recognition, fluency, and comprehension.* New York: Scholastic.

Rasinski, T. V., & Padak, N. D. 1998. How elementary students referred for compensatory reading instruction perform on school-based measures of word recognition, fluency, and comprehension. *Reading Psychology: An International Quarterly 19*: 185–216.

Rasinski, T. V., & Padak, N. 2004. *Effective Reading Strategies: Teaching Children who find Reading Difficult* (3rd Ed.). Columbus, OH: Merrill/Prentice Hall.

Rasinski, T. V,, & Padak, N. D. 2001. *From Phonics to Fluency: Effective Teaching of Decoding and Reading Fluency in the Elementary School.* New York: Longman.

Rasinski, T. V., Padak, N. D., Linek, W. L., & Sturtevant, E. 1994. Effects of fluency development on urban second-grade readers. *Journal of Educational Research 87*: 158–165.

Rasinski, T. V., & Zutell, J. B. 1996. Is fluency yet a goal of the reading curriculum? In E. G. Sturtevant & W. M. Linek (Eds.), *Growing literacy*: 18th Yearbook of the College Reading Association (pp. 237–246). Harrisonburg, VA: College Reading Association.

Reutzel, D.R., & Hollingsworth, P. M. 1993. Effects of fluency training on second graders' reading comprehension. *Journal of Educational Research 86*: 325–331.

Samuels, S. J. 1979. The method of repeated readings. *The Reading Teacher 32:* 403–408.

Schreiber, P. A. 1980. On the acquisition of reading fluency. *Journal of Reading Behavior 12*: 17–186.

Stahl, S., & Heubach, K. (in press). Fluency oriented reading instruction. *Elementary School Journal.*

Strecker, S., Roser, N., & Martinez, N. 1998. Toward an understanding of oral reading fluency. In T. Shanahan & F. Rodriguez-Brown (Eds.), *Forty-seventh Yearbook of the National Reading Conference* (pp. 295–310). Chicago: National Reading Conference.

Topping, K. 1989. Peer tutoring and paired reading. Combining two powerful techniques. *The Reading Teacher 42*: 488–494.

Topping, K. 1995. *Paired reading, spelling, and writing.* New York: Cassell.

Tyler, B. J., & Chard, D. 2000. Using readers theater to foster fluency in struggling readers: A twist on the repeated reading strategy. *Reading and Writing Quarterly 16*: 163–168.

Wheldall, K. 2000. Does Rainbow repeated reading add value to an intensive literacy intervention program for low-progress readers? An experimental evaluation. *Educational Review, 52(1)*: 29–36.

Wilkinson, I., Wardrop, J. L, & Anderson, R. C. 1988. Silent reading reconsidered: Reinterpreting reading instruction and its effects. *American Educational Research Journal 25*: 127–144.

Worthy, J., & Broaddus, K. 2002. Fluency beyond the primary grades: From group performance to silent, independent reading. *The Reading Teacher 55*: 334–343.

Worthy, J., & Prater, K. 2002. "I thought about it all night": Readers Theater for reading fluency and motivation. *The Reading Teacher 56*: 294–297.

Zutell, J. & Rasinski, T. V. 1991. Training teachers to attend to their students' oral reading fluency. *Theory into Practice 30*: 211–217.

Notes